Safe and Simple
Electrical Experiments

by
RUDOLF F. GRAF

DOVER PUBLICATIONS, INC.
NEW YORK

To my children Jeffrey and Debbie
Whose imagination and interest encouraged me to write this book
And to my wife Bettina
For her understanding and invaluable assistance

Published in Canada by General Publishing Company, Ltd., 30 Lesmill Road, Don Mills, Toronto, Ontario.
Published in the United Kingdom by Constable and Company, Ltd., 10 Orange Street, London WC2.

This Dover edition, first published in 1973, is an unabridged republication of the work originally published by John F. Rider Publisher, Inc., in 1964 under the title *The Safe and Simple Book of Electricity*.

International Standard Book Number: 0-486-22950-5
Library of Congress Catalog Card Number: 73-78175

Manufactured in the United States of America
Dover Publications, Inc.
180 Varick Street
New York, N. Y. 10014

PREFACE

The fastest and most reliable way of gaining a thorough understanding of electricity is by working with it and performing experiments rather than by just reading about it. With that thought in mind, I have prepared this book for the young and old alike who want to know about electricity but have little or no scientific experience.

This is not a reading book, nor a study book, yet it tells many interesting facts about electricity. It is not a picture book either, though it is full of illustrations. Rather this is a *doing* book! Every experiment has been tested numerous times so that if you follow the simple directions, you can count on spending many enjoyable hours successfully performing each of them. At the same time you will be learning many of the basic principles of electricity.

The book's uniform format makes it easy to follow. All experiments begin with a listing of the materials needed and a few introductory remarks. Detailed, step-by-step instructions allow you to set up most experiments in just a few minutes. These are followed by a brief discussion of the results you should expect.

In preparing this volume, I have avoided any experiments that require special or expensive materials which cannot be found in the average home or readily and cheaply obtained elsewhere. Furthermore, neither high voltages nor dangerous acids are needed for any of the experiments, nor do any require connections to the house current. All of them may be performed by even the most inexperienced or careless individual without the slightest possibility of doing harm to anyone. No special tools are needed, and the sizes of the wires, nails, and the like, that are used are not at all critical. Any size will do.

You will no doubt enjoy reading about the experiments, but you will not get the greatest pleasure nor reap the full benefit that this book can offer unless you actually do them. Since your success will depend to a large extent on the knowledge gained from previous experiments, it is best to perform them in the order in which they are presented.

Some of the experiments in this book, I must confess, have been adapted from the works of great scientists, but many are quite new and appear here for the first time. A number produce such astonishing results that they may even be used as stunts at the dinner table or at a party.

If it adds to your knowledge and understanding of electricity, this book will have served its intended purpose. As you progress, you will soon realize that no experiment is ever completely finished. Instead, the answers it provides you should only whet your appetite for embarking upon new and inviting explorations. Before long, you will discover the value of learning-by-doing. In time you should come to a thorough understanding of some of the basic forces of nature that affect you in a hundred different ways every day of your life.

As you venture forth into this new world of science, I wish you luck! With continuing interest in what is presented to you and with eagerness for what lies beyond, you may perhaps someday be the Volta of the future.

RUDOLF F. GRAF

P.S. If you should originate or know of an unusual experiment that might be included in this book, please be so kind as to drop me a note about it in care of the publisher. It might make a welcome addition to a future edition.

CONTENTS

A Brief Chronological History of Great Discoveries in Electricity

2637 B.C.

Hoang-ti, founder of the Chinese empire, uses a magnetic chariot (legend).

600 B.C.

Thales of Miletus (640-546), Greek scientist and philosopher, discovers attractive power of charged amber.

1269 A.D.

Petrus Peregrinus discovers properties of magnetism and shows that like poles (his own term) repel and unlike poles attract.

1492

Christopher Columbus (1451-1506) shows that the declination of a compass needle varies for different parts of the world.

1600

William Gilbert (1540-1603), English physician and physicist, publishes *De Magnete,* six volumes describing the earth as having the properties of a huge magnet (and thereby explaining the behavior of the compass needle). Gilbert also coined the word "electricity" from "electron," the Greek word for amber.

1650

Otto van Guericke (1602-1686), German physicist, builds the first static machine. Consisting of a large sulphur ball mounted on a shaft, this machine produced static electricity when a pad was rubbed against the ball as it rotated.

1729

Stephen Gray (1696-1736), English electrical experimenter, evolves the concept of conductors and nonconductors. His theory led to the discovery of electrical insulation.

1733

Charles François de Cisternay Du Fay (1698-1739) of Paris discovers that there are only two kinds of electricity — vitreous (positive) and resinous (negative) — and announces that like charges repel and unlike charges attract.

1745

Pieter van Musschenbroek (1692-1761), Dutch mathematician, discovers principle of the Leyden jar, wherein charges of static electricity can be built up and stored.

1747

Benjamin Franklin (1706-1790), American statesman and philosopher, advances single fluid theory of electricity, originates "plus" and "minus" designations, and invents the lightning rod.

1771

Luigi Galvani (1737-1798), Italian physiologist, discovers that a frog's legs contract when touched at different points by two dissimilar metals which also touch. Galvani advanced theory of "animal electricity" in 1786.

1785

Charles Augustin de Coulomb (1736-1806), French physicist, proves the law of inverse squares, which states that the force exerted between two charged spheres is directly proportional to the product of their charges and is inversely proportional to the square of the distance between them. Coulomb also proved that the internal surface of a body cannot be charged with static electricity.

1800

Allesandro Volta (1745-1827), Italian physicist, discovers the first practical method of generating electricity. The voltaic pile (named in his honor) consists of a stack of silver and zinc plates separated from each other by cloth or paper saturated with a salt solution.

1819

Hans Christian Oersted (1777-1851), Danish physicist, discovers that a magnetic field is caused by electric current, thus proving that electricity and magnetism are related.

1820

André Marie Ampère (1775-1836), French physicist, shows that the forces between currents and magnets and also between two currents can be determined by assuming that each element of the circuit exerts a force on a magnetic pole and on every other current element in the circuit. This discovery established the relationship between electricity and magnetism. Ampère also developed the solenoid.

1820

Dominique François Jean Arago (1786-1853), French physicist, discovers that a magnet can be made from an iron or steel bar placed inside a solenoid through which current is flowing.

1821

Michael Faraday (1791-1867), English chemist and physicist, shows that the flow of current in a wire can cause a magnet to revolve around the wire and that a current-carrying wire tends to revolve around a fixed magnet.

1823

Thomas Johann Seebeck (1770-1831), German physicist, discovers that an electric current is produced when two dissimilar metals are joined and their junction point is heated.

1827

Georg Simon Ohm (1787-1854), German physicist, discovers the relation between current, voltage, and resistance in an electric circuit, now known as Ohm's law, which states that the electromotive force divided by the rate of current flow through a conductor represents the resistance of the conductor.

1831

Joseph Henry (1797-1878), professor of physics in Albany, N. Y., and Michael Faraday make numerous electromagnetic discoveries, such as the principle of self-inductance, the transformer, the generation of electricity by magnetism, the disk dynamo, and many others.

1833

Karl Friedrich Gauss (1777-1855), German physicist and mathematician, develops an exact mathematical formula for the magnetic field.

1834

Heinrich Friedrich Emil Lenz (1804-1865), German-Russian physicist, establishes a method of determining the directions of an induced current in a circuit, now known as Lenz's law.

1840

Samuel F. B. Morse (1791-1872), American artist and inventor, invents the telegraph.

1859

Gaston Planté (1834-1899), French inventor, makes first lead-acid storage cell to store electrical energy.

1865

James Clerk Maxwell (1831-1879), Scottish physicist, explains in mathematical terms the transmission of electric and magnetic fields through a medium.

1875

Alexander Graham Bell (1847-1922), American inventor, develops the electric telephone.

1879

Thomas Alva Edison (1847-1931), American inventor, develops a dynamo and the incandescent lamp. Edison also invented the phonograph, an improved telegraph system, talking pictures, the alkaline storage battery, and many other electrical devices.

1887

Heinrich Rudolph Hertz (1857-1894), German physicist, discovers that certain metals give off electric energy when struck by light. Herz also discovered in 1888 that electricity may be transmitted by electromagnetic waves.

1888

Nicola Tesla (1856-1943), American engineer and inventor, announces discovery of the principle of the rotating magnetic field, on which the induction motor is based.

1895

Guglielmo Marconi (1874-1937), Italian inventor, begins experiments in wireless telegraphy.

A word of explanation: The reason we stop our chronology at this point is that by the time of the invention of wireless telegraphy, the basic principles of electricity had been formulated. Beyond them lies the field of electronics, a subject outside the scope of this book.

static electricity

Early History of Static Electricity

Thousands of years ago pine trees grew along the shores of the Baltic Sea. Although they slowly disappeared and are now long extinct, the gum from their bark became petrified and still exists. It is called amber. The ancient Greeks used amber to make necklaces and other forms of jewelry.

The Greek philosopher Thales of Miletus, reckoned to be among the Seven Wise Men of Greece, is credited with having been the first to record that a piece of amber rubbed against fur or clothing will sparkle and also attract dried leaves, feathers, pith, lint, and the like. We don't know whether this curious phenomenon was ever noticed before his time, but Thales was the first to mark it down for posterity. That was about 2,500 years ago (between 640 and 546 B.C.). It was an interesting discovery, but nobody was then able to explain exactly what was happening, and for hundreds of years the "magic" power of attraction was regarded simply as an interesting natural event.

For a long time this curious effect was associated only with amber, but later on rubbed glass was found to have similar if somewhat opposite properties. Thus there were said to be two kinds of electricity. The kind exhibited by rubbed glass was called "vitreous" and the kind exhibited by rubbed amber was called "resinous." In the Middle Ages it was discovered that many other substances showed similar properties when rubbed. These were collectively called "electrics." Those substances which could not be given this property by rubbing were then called "nonelectrics." "Electrics" are actually insulators or nonconductors, whereas "nonelectrics" are conductors. To avoid confusion, both of these terms were dropped at a later date.

Little more was discovered about this mysterious attraction until Sir William Gilbert of England, at the turn of the seventeenth century, continued where Thales left off. He published a book in which he described his work and is credited with having coined the word "electricity" from "electron" (the Greek word for amber.) Other scientists became interested, and by careful and painstaking investigation they slowly were able to unlock nature's secrets to help us arrive at a better understanding of electricity.

Electricity as we now know it is of two basic kinds: static electricity and current electricity. Static electricity is the kind that Thales discovered by rubbing amber and that others discovered by rubbing glass. Its name comes from the Greek word meaning "standing," because it is normally at rest. It passes from one body to another only in sudden, momentary movements. Of limited usefulness, it is often a nuisance and a hazard that can cause fires and take lives. Nonetheless, when controlled, we can have some fun with it and learn a great deal about electricity at the same time.

Static electricity experiments work best when the weather is cool and dry. Cold winter days, when the air inside is dry and warm, are ideal. On damp summer days the electrons are likely to flow away instead of staying where you can study them. Therefore if you have difficulty with any of the experiments in this section on static electricity, try it again on a day when there is less moisture in the air. On the other hand, on a very dry day, the static electricity you yourself produce by rubbing your shoes on a wool or nylon rug can also interfere with your experiment. On such days spread newspaper under your feet. Remember again, all of these experiments have been performed many times, and if you have followed directions carefully and any of them fail to work, you can most assuredly blame it on the weather.

Charge Yourself

Materials you will need:

1. *Woolen rug on the floor*
2. *Fluorescent tube*

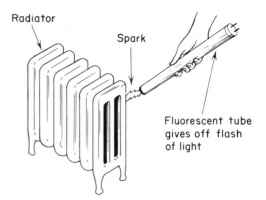

Radiator

Spark

Fluorescent tube gives off flash of light

IF you ever got a shock on a cool winter day when you reached for a door knob or shook somebody's hand, you may have wondered what happened. In a darkened room you may have seen a spark. If your radio was turned on, you may even have heard the static you broadcast when the spark jumped. This is the same kind of interference you get from lightning. As a matter of fact the little spark and lightning have a lot in common.

No one knows exactly what static electricity is, and no one knows all the reasons why charged objects behave the way they do, but scientists have developed a theory that explains most of these actions. All substances are said to be made of positive electrical particles called *protons* and negative electrical particles called *electrons*. When an object is left undisturbed for a period of time the protons and electrons balance each other. That object has no charge and is said to be *neutral*. When some objects are rubbed they pick up electrons from the material doing the rubbing, whereas others give electrons to the material rubbed against them. The objects are then said to be negatively or positively charged. More on this later.

Now for our first experiment. Rub your shoes on the rug to pick up and accumulate electrons on your body. Then touch something, especially something made of metal. These excess electrons will now leave you and jump to the metal. That is what you feel, and that is the spark you see. Once this spark has jumped, you no longer have any electrical charge. To prove this, touch the object again. You will feel no more shock because all the electrical charge (electrons) you had is no longer there. Shuffle your feet again to pick up more charges and you can repeat the process.

Now try this: While holding a fluorescent tube, charge yourself well by rubbing your shoes on the rug. To make the tube give off a brief flash of light, touch the metal end to a radiator or the screw of a light switch plate while holding the tube in your hand. The tube will flash briefly as *your* charge passes through it to the radiator.

If you cannot produce a charge on a cool dry day, it is probably due to the fact that your rug has been treated with some antistatic material.

Charge a Balloon

Materials you will need:

1. *Rubber balloon*
2. *Piece of wool or fur*

BLOW up a balloon, tie its neck securely, and rub it quickly and vigorously against a piece of wool. A sweater or a jacket is ideal for this purpose. Now hold the balloon up

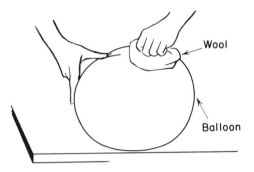

against the wall. It will stick to it. It will also stick to your hand, a table, or even the ceiling if you can throw it up so that it just reaches the ceiling and does not bounce back too vigorously.

The explanation of this reaction is that rubbing removed some of the free electrons from the wool and moved them onto the balloon. This gave the balloon a negative charge. When this charged balloon was brought next to an uncharged object, such as the wall, it repelled the electrons away from the wall nearest the balloon, since like charges repel. Now there was an attraction between the balloon and the positive charges left on the wall nearest the balloon.

Once the balloons are charged, they will stick to any uncharged body and will also stick to any person anywhere on his body. Some rather amusing sights can thus be produced.

Charge a number of balloons, and you can actually walk around with the balloons clinging to you.

After a while, depending on the humidity in the air, the charge on the balloon will leak off by itself. If you want to be sure at any time that a balloon is completely discharged, put it under running water and then hang it up to dry. The water will wash away all the charges.

Blow up another balloon, charge it the same way, and try to stick it right next to the balloon on the wall. You will see that the two balloons will repel each other, and though they both will stick to the wall, they will be separated by some distance and never touch each other.

Here is something else you can try. Put a good charge on your balloon, and hold it close to your ear. You will hear crackling noises that sound very much like static on a radio receiver. This noise is caused by very tiny sparks that jump between your body and the charged balloon.

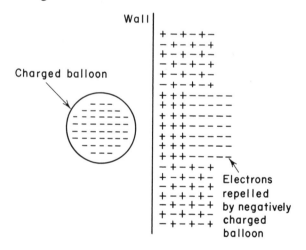

Charge a Piece of Paper

Materials you will need:

1. *Sheet of paper*
2. *Wool, nylon, Saran wrap*

BY simply rubbing a piece of paper on a dry day, it can be charged with static electricity. Hold a piece of dry paper against a wall with one hand, and rub it briskly with the other hand for a few seconds. The friction will charge the paper and make it stick to the wall. It is held there by the attraction between the charged paper and the neutral wall, as explained before. On a dry day, the paper will stick to the wall for several hours. Lift one corner of the paper slightly, and let it go. It will snap back into place, being again attracted to the wall.

Pull the paper completely away from the wall, and you will hear a crackling sound caused by the sparks which fly from the charged paper to the wall. The paper is still charged, and if you place it against another spot on the wall, a door, or a window pane, it will once more be held in place. Hold the charged paper near your face, and it will produce a tickling sensation.

A greater charge can be placed on the paper if you rub it with some of the following materials rather than with your hand. Try fur, wool, nylon, and Saran wrap, and see which gives you the greatest charge.

As a further experiment, place some celluloid or Saran wrap against the wall, and rub

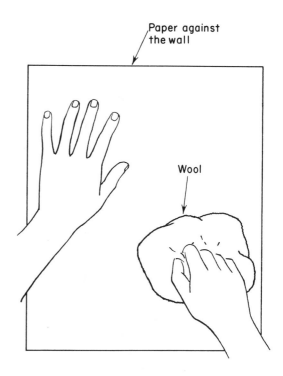

it with nylon or wool. You will build up some very great charges with these materials, and the results will be quite interesting.

Tricks with a Comb

4

Materials you will need:
1. *Plastic comb*
2. *Piece of wool or nylon*
3. *Tiny bits of paper and/or a cup full of puffed rice*
4. *Some cigarette ashes*

TEAR some very tiny bits of paper, and place them on a table. Now rub the comb vigorously with a piece of wool or nylon (as shown in Figure A), and bring the comb close to the tiny pieces of paper. You will see that the paper will be attracted by the comb, but

watch what happens after a while. A few of the pieces of paper will suddenly shoot off the comb. First one and then another and then another. For a really interesting effect, plunge the charged comb into the puffed rice, and quickly pull it out. A lot of the puffed rice will cling to the comb, but in an instant, the grains will begin to pop off as if shot from a gun. What happened there? Why were these objects first attracted and then repelled?

What we have done by rubbing the comb is to give it a strong negative charge. Being charged, the comb attracts the uncharged bits

Puffed rice

Charged comb

Because neither the paper nor the puffed rice is a good conductor, it takes a little time for the electrons to transfer from the comb. When this transfer is complete, the object suddenly jumps off.

Make a small pile of cigarette ashes and bring the charged comb close to it. Some of the ashes will fly up to the comb and, after being in contact with it for an instant, will fly off again. What happened here is the same thing that happened before. The ashes acquired a negative charge on the comb, and since like charges repel, the ashes fly off very rapidly.

of paper or puffed rice, as the case may be. As soon as the little objects make contact with the comb, they acquire some of its negative charge. Since the comb also is negatively charged and we know that like charges repel, the object will fly off once it has acquired its charge.

You can repeat the same experiments with a charged glass rod, and the effect will be the same. This time, though, instead of the paper, puffed rice, or ashes acquiring negative charges from the negatively charged comb, they will acquire positive charges from the positively charged rod.

5 Drawing Sparks from a Dry Newspaper

Materials you will need:

1. *Sheet of newspaper*
2. *Polyethylene sheet or bag (the kind used to wrap vegetables, or used as a protective cover over clothes coming from the cleaners)*
3. *Piece of wool*
4. *Old nylon stocking*
5. *Smooth, round top from a can, or the metal top from a pry-off glass jar, at least 3 inches in diameter.*

IT is possible to draw a nice sized spark from an electrified piece of paper. To do so, place a dry sheet of newspaper on a table, and rub it vigorously with the polyethylene for about 15 to 30 seconds to give the paper a strong electrostatic charge. Then put the round metal piece in the center of the paper, and lift the paper off the table by holding it on both sides as shown. Now, if someone else quickly comes close to the metal disc with his finger, he will draw a nice spark. On a dry day, you should be able to draw a spark of about a quarter inch or so, which would represent a charge of approximately 10,000 volts. Nevertheless, the spark is harmless. If the paper is completely dry and the weather favorable, the spark may be fully an inch long. (To be sure the paper is absolutely dry, place it in a warm over for about a half hour.)

Rub the paper again, but this time use the nylon stocking. Place the disk on it, lift the paper, and see how big a spark you can now draw. Repeat the same experiment with the wool to find out which of the three materials gives the highest charge, as indicated by the longest spark that can be drawn.

Sheet of newspaper   Top of can

Fill the Stocking

> **Materials you will need:**
>
> 1. *Nylon stocking*
> 2. *Polyethylene bag*

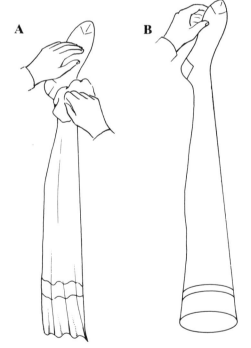

A   B

HERE is how you can fill out a nylon stocking simply by rubbing it. Hold the toe of the stocking against the wall with one hand, and with the other hand rub over it with the polyethylene bag, as shown in Figure A. (You can tell that the bag is made of polyethylene material if it can be easily stretched.)

After about five or ten strokes, pull the stocking from the wall and hold it in the air. The stocking quickly fills out, making it look as if it were actually filled with an invisible leg (Figure B). Why does this happen?

We found out before that like charges repel each other. When we rubbed the stocking with the polyethylene material, we put a very strong charge on it, so that its sides now repel each other and try to get as far apart as possible. Thus the stocking fills out.

At the same time that we charged the stocking we also put an opposite charge on the polyethylene bag. If you bring the bag close to the stocking, they will be attracted towards each other (unlike charges attract).

[7]

7

Making Water Wiggle

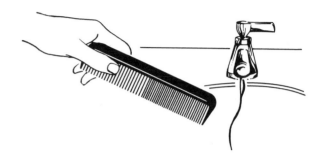

GET a *very fine, continuous* stream of water from a cold water faucet. Charge the comb by rubbing it briskly with the wool, and bring it close to the thin stream of water. Watch what happens as you get closer. As if by magic, the stream bends towards the charged comb. You can move the comb all around, and the stream will seem to wiggle like a snake.

As soon as you let the water touch the comb, the comb loses its deflecting power. It must be *dried well* and recharged by rubbing before the experiment can be done again.

What happened was this: The negatively charged comb attracted the neutral stream of water and deflected it. As soon as the comb got wet, its charge leaked off through the water.

8

The Obedient Ping Pong Ball

PLACE a ping pong ball on a smooth, level table surface so that it can freely roll in any direction. Then rub the comb brisky with the woolen piece so that it acquires a good charge. Bring the charged comb close to the ping pong ball, and watch what happens. The uncharged ball is attracted by the charged comb and starts to roll towards it.

When this happens, don't let the ball touch the comb, but move the comb away, and you will see that the ball will follow it obed-

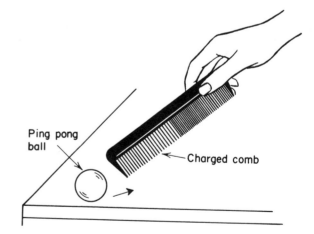

Ping pong ball

Charged comb

iently all over the table. For the best results, approach the ball with the flat side of the comb (see illustration), and be ready to move as soon as the ball starts rolling.

How to Break Up a Friendship Between Two Balloons

> **Materials you will need:**
>
> 1. *Two rubber balloons*
> 2. *Some wool or fur*
> 3. *Four feet of silk or nylon thread*

BLOW up two rubber balloons and tie their necks securely so that they remain inflated. Hang them on a piece of silk or nylon thread about two feet long. We use a thread because it is a good insulator and the charges put on our balloons will not leak away readily.

Charge both of the balloons as we have done previously by rubbing them with the wool or a piece of fur. Then hold the balloons by their strings, one string in each hand. Now try to make the balloons touch each other by bringing your hands together. You will never be able to do it. The balloons will push each other apart, as if some invisible force were pushing them away from each other.

Here is what is happening. When we rubbed the balloons, each acquired negative charges. Both have the same charge and therefore repel each other.

With the balloons still charged, hold both strings in one hand. The balloons should still repel each other. Bring the other hand near one of the balloons. It will be attracted towards the hand, but don't let it touch. If you put your hand between both balloons, they will come together and touch the hand. What is happening here is this. The negatively charged balloons approach the uncharged hand because the negative charges in the hand are repelled by the negative charges on the balloon. This leaves the hand with a net positive charge that attracts the oppositely charged balloons. This

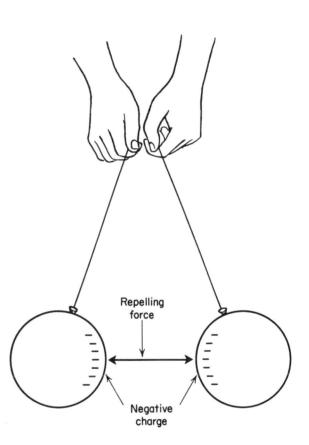

attraction is sufficient to hold the balloon to the hand.

If you suspend the charged balloons in a doorway in which there is a slight draft, they will keep on spinning around each other but will never touch until their charges have leaked off. Now that you have seen what happens with two balloons, try the same experiment with three balloons. The way they try to avoid each other presents a very amusing spectacle indeed.

Bringing Two Balloons Back Together

Materials you will need:

1. *Two rubber balloons*
2. *Some wool or fur*
3. *Saran wrap*
4. *Four feet of silk or nylon thread*

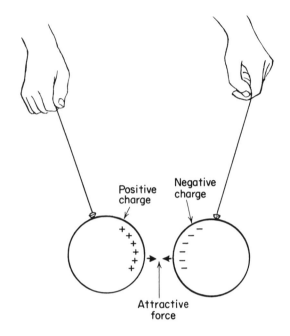

Positive charge

Negative charge

Attractive force

BLOW up two balloons, tie their necks securely, and attach each to a 2-foot piece of silk or nylon thread. Then rub one balloon against the wool, and rub the other balloon with a piece of Saran wrap. Now hold the balloons by their strings, one string in each hand, so that they hang straight down. First hold them quite far apart, then bring them closer together, and note what happens. The balloons will be strongly attracted to each other, and if you let them come close enough, they will eventually touch. As soon as they do touch, they will be neutral again and hang down straight.

Here's why: That balloon which has an excess of electrons (the one rubbed with the fur or wool) gave up its electrons to the balloon with a shortage of electrons (the one charged with the Saran wrap). As a result of this transfer of electrons when the balloons touched, there was no longer an excess of electrons on the one balloon and no deficiency of electrons on the other. There being no further attraction or repulsion between them, they hang down straight.

Like Charges Repel

Materials you will need:

1. *Two strips of newspaper, each about 1 inch wide and 20 inches long*
2. *Polyethylene bag, nylon stocking, or piece of wool*

YOU can make strips of newspaper fly apart simply by rubbing them. Hold the strips at one end, and let them hang down as shown. You will see that they hang down straight, one next to the other. Now stroke them lengthwise, from top to bottom, with the thumb and forefinger of the free hand. After several strokes they will have acquired a charge. Since both of the strips have the same charge, and we know that like charges repel, they will fly apart.

An even greater charge can be put on these strips, and thus much wider separation obtained, by rubbing them with a piece of polyethylene, such as that used in a cleaner or vegetable bag, or with some wool. Make sure that the outside surfaces of the strips both get rubbed at the same time. Either of these materials will produce a greater charge much faster, so that now the strips will really fly apart, oftentimes after just one stroke.

The charges which were placed on the paper strips as well as on the material we used for charging them will be very readily indicated on the electroscope or charge indicator that we will build in the next experiment.

For further experimentation, try rubbing the strips with other materials, and see which produces the greatest charge. You can also try the same experiment with three or more strips, and you will really see some interesting effects.

To show that charges distribute all over the strips, reverse them. That is, bring the bottoms of the two strips which are now apart together, hold them together, and bring them to the top. Conversely, drop the two ends which were previously held up, and release

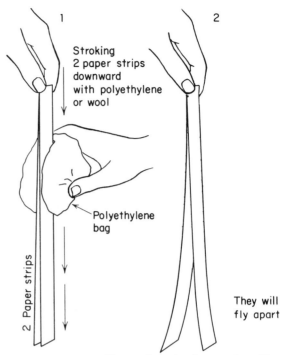

them. Now you will see that the free ends will again fly apart.

Building and Using a Leaf Electroscope 12

Materials you will need:

1. *Small bottle (milk bottle will also do)*
2. *Large paper clip or stiff piece of wire (approximately 6 inches long)*
3. *About ½ square foot of aluminum or tin foil*
4. *Chewing gum wrapper or other source of thin metal foil*
5. *Rubber or cork stopper to fit the opening of the bottle used*

AN electroscope is an easily constructed and very useful instrument for determining the presence of electrostatic charges. It indicates the existence of charges on anything we bring near it, and it will also tell us the polarity of the charges — that is, whether they are positive or negative. From our previous experiment

with the newspaper strips, we know that if we hold two light narrow strips together at one end and give them the same charge, the free ends will fly apart. The electroscope basically consists of the lightest metal foils (or leaves as they are also called) we can find, placed inside some sort of container such as a bottle. The bottle is needed to assure that the sensitive foils are not disturbed by air currents. Construction of the electroscope is very simple and can be accomplished in just a few minutes.

First of all, shape a paper clip or piece of wire with an L-shaped appendage as shown in Figure A and push it through the stopper that fits the bottle you are using. It is most important that both the stopper and the bottle be completely dry. To be sure that they are, dry them in a warm oven for a little while just before you are ready to assemble the electroscope.

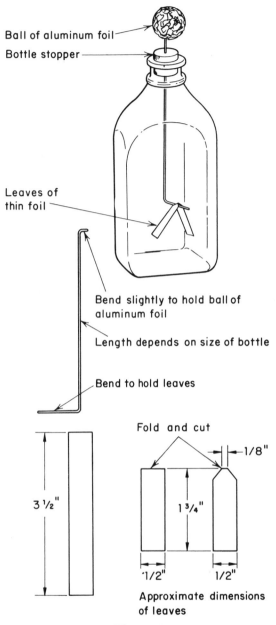

Ball of aluminum foil

Bottle stopper

Leaves of thin foil

Bend slightly to hold ball of aluminum foil

Length depends on size of bottle

Bend to hold leaves

Fold and cut

1/8"

3 ½"

1 ³/₄"

1/2"   1/2"

Approximate dimensions of leaves

Figure A

About a half inch of the paper clip or wire should be left protruding from the stopper to hold a ball of aluminum foil. This ball should be as round as possible for best results. It is made by packing and squeezing aluminum foil into a little sphere, which is then simply pushed onto the wire.

The leaves are made from the lightest available material. A strip of tissue paper will serve in a pinch, but the foil from a stick of chewing gum is best for our purpose. The paper can be separated from the foil by soaking the wrapper in warm water for a few minutes. The foil and paper will then come apart easily. Straighten the foil, dry it, and cut a strip about ½ inch wide and 3½ inches long. In order to make the instrument as sensitive as possible, the leaves should be able to separate with the least resistance, so make them extremely narrow at the point at which they rest on the support.

To do this, fold the strip in half (lengthwise) and cut off a little triangle from either side of the fold so as to leave only a very narrow bridge. Then lay the leaves onto the L-shaped section of the wire. The leaves should be straightened out so that they will hang loosely and parallel to each other. Now insert the cork with all its attachments into the bottle, and the electroscope is finished. For best results be sure that everything is dry — absolutely dry. Otherwise charges will leak off very rapidly, and you may not be able to charge your electroscope at all.

Here is how the electroscope works. If it is touched with a charged object, the charges will run down the wire into the leaves, both of which will get identical charges. Since we know that like charges repel, the leaves will fly apart at the bottom because they are hinged together at the top. Now to use our electroscope.

Rub a comb briskly for about 30 seconds with a piece of nylon (an old nylon stocking will be fine) to give the comb a negative charge. If you bring it *close* to the knob of the electroscope, the leaves will separate. When the comb is taken away, they will return to their normal position. If you *touch* the knob with the comb, the electroscope will acquire a negative charge, and it will remain charged even after the comb is removed. We have charged the electroscope by *contact* (Figure B). Touching the knob with the finger offers an easy escape path for the negative charge which has been put on the electroscope, and thus the electroscope is discharged.

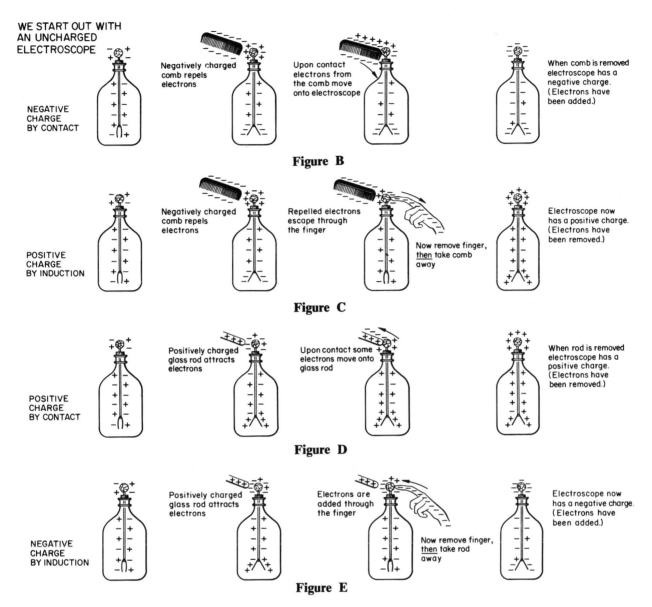

WE START OUT WITH AN UNCHARGED ELECTROSCOPE

NEGATIVE CHARGE BY CONTACT

Negatively charged comb repels electrons

Upon contact electrons from the comb move onto electroscope

When comb is removed electroscope has a negative charge. (Electrons have been added.)

Figure B

POSITIVE CHARGE BY INDUCTION

Negatively charged comb repels electrons

Repelled electrons escape through the finger

Now remove finger, *then* take comb away

Electroscope now has a positive charge. (Electrons have been removed.)

Figure C

POSITIVE CHARGE BY CONTACT

Positively charged glass rod attracts electrons

Upon contact some electrons move onto glass rod

When rod is removed electroscope has a positive charge. (Electrons have been removed.)

Figure D

NEGATIVE CHARGE BY INDUCTION

Positively charged glass rod attracts electrons

Electrons are added through the finger

Now remove finger, *then* take rod away

Electroscope now has a negative charge. (Electrons have been added.)

Figure E

To give our electroscope a positive charge, bring the same charged comb near the knob, and with a finger of the other hand touch the knob for about a second. In doing so, we allow a few additional positive charges to travel from our finger to the knob of the electroscope. Take the hand away from the knob, and *then* remove the comb. You'll note that as the comb is removed, the two leaves will separate (Figure C). We have now charged the electroscope by *induction* with a positive charge. Bringing the charged comb near the knob of the electroscope once more will cause the leaves to return to their normal position, and

they will separate again as soon as the comb is removed, providing you have not touched the knob of the electroscope.

To give the electroscope a positive charge *by contact,* touch the knob with a positively charged glass rod as shown in Figure D. To give it a negative charge *by induction,* proceed as in Figure E.

The electroscope can also be used to determine unknown charges. Here is how: First charge the electroscope with a known charge. Let us assume that we have charged it by contact with a comb rubbed with nylon so that it will now have a negative charge. If we bring the object whose charge is not known near the ball of the charged electroscope, one of two things will happen. The leaves will either separate more or come closer together. If the object is negatively charged, it will repel the electrons on the ball of the electroscope and send them down towards the leaves, thereby causing them to separate even more. On the other hand, if the object is positively charged, it will attract some of the electrons away from the leaves towards the ball. This will cause the leaves to come closer together, since they are not charged so strongly any more.

The same action will occur, but with opposite charges, if we give the electroscope a positive charge, as we did above. In this case the leaves will separate more if a positively charged object is brought near the electroscope and will come closer together if we approach the ball with a negatively charged object.

How far the leaves separate gives us a direct indication of the relative amount of charge which is placed on the electroscope. Thus the farther they spread apart, the greater the charge. The charge on the electroscope can be accumulated by charging it several times from the same charged object or from another having a charge of the same polarity (positive or negative). The leaves will thus spead farther apart each time an additional charge is put on the electroscope. Before starting any new experiments, always discharge the electroscope first by touching its metal ball with your finger.

Charge the electroscope by contact and by induction from various other objects to become familiar with this simple but important instrument. Make a note of the different amount of charge that various objects produce.

13 Discharging Your Electroscope by Radiation or Ionization

Materials you will need:

1. *Leaf electroscope*
2. *Watch or clock with radiant dial*
3. *Matches (and candle)*

A CHARGED electroscope will become discharged if the air around it can be made conductive. This can be done by placing the electroscope in the vicinity of X-rays or some radioactive material. Hold the radium dial of a clock or a watch several inches from the knob of the charged electroscope and see how quickly it discharges. For best results, the crystal of the timepiece should be removed to permit easier passage of the alpha rays which it otherwise obstructs.

Objects can thus be easily tested for radio-activity by bringing them close to the knob of an electroscope or by actually putting them into the bottle. If the electroscope remains charged for a relatively long time but discharges more rapidly when the object under test is near it, then the object is radioactive. If no effects are noted, then the object is not radioactive.

We can also discharge the electroscope with a lighted candle or a match. When a gas (such as air) is heated, the speed of its molecules increases and ionization is more likely to occur, that is, the molecules are more likely to become positively or negatively charged. Bring a lighted candle or a match near the ball of the charged electroscope, and you will see that again the leaves will close. The charges have indeed leaked off into the ionized, or charged, air. Now try an interesting experiment.

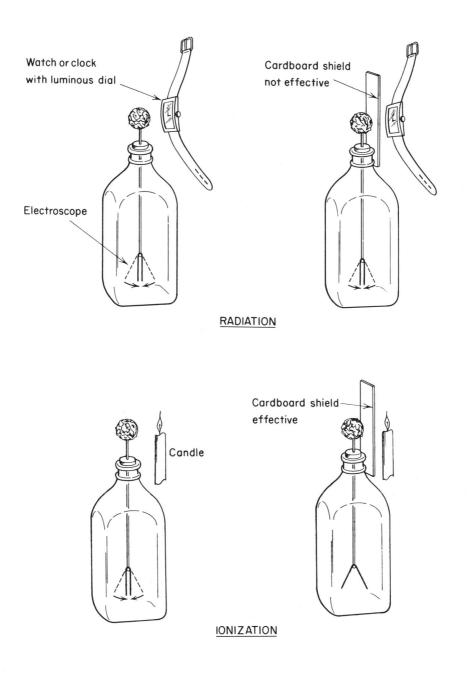

Watch or clock
with luminous dial

Electroscope

RADIATION

Cardboard shield
not effective

Candle

Cardboard shield
effective

IONIZATION

Hold a piece of cardboard between the candle and the knob of the electroscope, and you will see that the flame will now have no more effect on the charged electroscope. The cardboard acts as a screen. Try to do the same shielding with the radioactive material. Does it also work? It does not! The cardboard does not act as a shield because those rays or particles emitted by the radioactive material are harder to stop and pass very easily through the cardboard.

Building an Electrophorus

Materials you will need:

1. *Candle or a glass rod*
2. *Old phonograph record (vinylite LP or shellac)*
3. *Piece of flannel or wool*
4. *Flat unpainted metal disk about 3 to 5 inches in diameter (this can be either the top from a can or, better yet, the top from a screw-top or twist-top jar)*

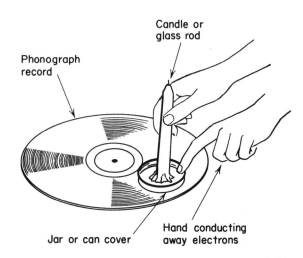

Candle or glass rod

Phonograph record

Jar or can cover

Hand conducting away electrons

IN 1775 Alessandro Volta constructed a device called an *electrophorus* which was capable of producing a great number of successive charges of static electricity. We can quickly and easily put together a modern-day electrophorus and produce high electrostatic charges and respectable sparks.

Heat the flat end of a candle with a match and let a good bit of wax drip onto the center of the metal disk. Then press the candle down, and hold it still until the wax is hard. The candle will now serve as an insulating handle for the charge-carrying disk. A more efficient handle (because it is a better insulator) is a short glass rod which can be held to the disk by wax drippings, modeling clay, or quick-drying cement, but the candle will also work. The edges of the disk must be smooth and have no sharp points; otherwise the charges will leak off by themselves very rapidly.

Place the record on a flat surface, and rub it vigorously with a piece of flannel or wool for about 30 seconds over an area at least the size of the charge-carrying disk. Place the charge-carrying disk on the record area which was just rubbed, and touch the disk with the finger of the other hand for just a moment. Then lift the disk by the handle, being careful not to touch the wick (if you use a candle) since that may cause some of the charges to leak off. The disk is now positively charged. If you bring it close to the knuckle of the other hand, a spark jumps from the knuckle to the disk. As a matter

of fact, the spark will jump to any part of the body, a radiator, a doorknob, or the like, so long as the disk is held by its insulating handle and has not been discharged.

The disk can be recharged time and again with only one rubbing of the phonograph record. When the sparks become weak, the record must be recharged by rubbing it several more times with the material to give it an additional charge.

When we place a metal plate which is a conductor on a negatively charged phonograph record, why don't we end up with a negatively rather than a positively charged disk? Here is why: Rubbing the record surface gave it a negative charge, but since it has many grooves it does not present a flat surface. When we put the neutral (uncharged) disk on the record, it makes contact with the disk in only a few high spots. There is actually no physical contact between the record and the disk over the greatest area, so that a positive charge will be *induced* in the disk's lower surface because it is closest to the phonograph record. Since we started out with a neutral disk, we have free, excess negative charges on the other surface. These are conducted away when that surface is touched by the finger. The record was charged negatively by contact when we generated frictional electricity, but the disk was charged positively by induction.

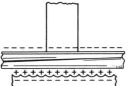
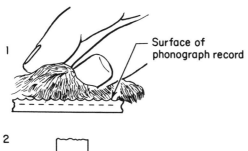

1. Rubbing record surface with fur gives it a strong negative charge

2. Placing charge carrying disk on charged record forces electrons to top of the disk

Surface of phonograph record

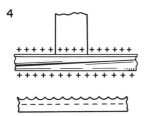

3. Finger on disk lets electrons move away to ground, leaving disk positively charged

4. Disk removed from phonograph record is now heavily positive. Bringing it near knuckle or discharging it through a neon bulb neutralizes the charge. It can be recharged a number of times by repeating steps 2 to 4

Using the Electrophorus 15

Materials you will need:

1. *Electrophorus (previously constructed)*
2. *Fluorescent bulb*
3. *Neon bulb*

THE charge from the electrophorus can be used to produce a flash of light in a fluorescent lamp. Every fluorescent bulb has metal end caps on each end. Hold the fluorescent bulb at one end of the end caps with one hand, and bring the charged disk to the other end cap. You will note that a spark will jump, and the bulb will light up briefly. For best effects, this experiment should be carried out in a darkened room. A burned out fluorescent bulb will work just as well as a new one.

The charges generated by the electrophorus can also be dissipated through a neon bulb of the type found in circuit testers or voltage indicators. A little plug-in night-light neon bulb will also work equally well. Hold any one of the terminals of the neon bulb, and bring the charge carrying disk near the other terminal. You will note a brief flash of light in the bulb as the discharge takes place. Now reverse and hold the other terminal. The bulb will flash as before.

Lay the neon bulb on a table, and bring the charged disk close to it without touching any of the wires. The bulb will glow (before you touch it), showing the effect of the strong electrostatic field around it.

The electrophorus can also be used to charge or to indicate the polarity of the charge on a leaf electroscope. Exercise great care not to *touch* the electroscope with the disk. The charge is much too high to be applied directly. The leaves would fly apart violently and perhaps tear off if such a great charge were put on them.

Another interesting experiment can be conducted using the electrophorus. Cut some

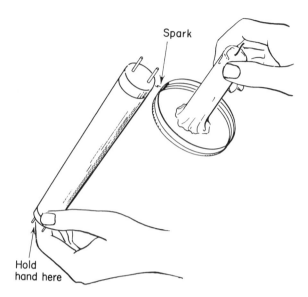

Spark

Hold hand here

very small pieces (about ½ x ½ inch) of paper from a piece of tissue paper in the shapes of fish, bugs, birds, or butterflies. Breathe on them slightly, lay them on top of the uncharged electrophorus disk, and then charge it. When you lift it off the record, watch what happens. The little bits of paper will, if they are not too wet, fly off the disk in a very short while. Here's why: After we charged our disk, the little pieces of paper acquired a charge from the disk. Since like charges repel, and they now have the same charge as the disk, they are repelled by it and, being very light, fly away.

16 Shielding Your Electroscope

Materials you will need:

1. *Leaf electroscope (made earlier)*
2. *Metal pot large enough to contain electroscope*
3. *Wire strainer to fit over pot and electroscope*

LIGHTNING is a huge spark that results when electrostatic charges jump from one cloud to another or from a cloud to a ground.

We are all familiar with this dangerous discharge. The best way to protect yourself against an electrostatic charge of any kind, including lightning, is to be completely enclosed inside a conductor or a frame made of conducting material. We know that like charges repel each other; therefore any electrostatic charges will always remain on the outside surface of such an enclosure. We can show that electrostatic charges cannot penetrate such a shield.

Place a charged electroscope inside a pot

covered with a wire strainer in such a manner as to form a complete shield around the electroscope. You can bring any charged material near, even the heavily charged disk of your electrophorus, and there will be no effect whatsoever on the electroscope. Even if you touch the screen or pot, nothing will happen. We have completely shielded the electroscope from any outside electrostatic charges. Any charges the pot or wire strainer may acquire will repel each other and thus remain on the outside surface.

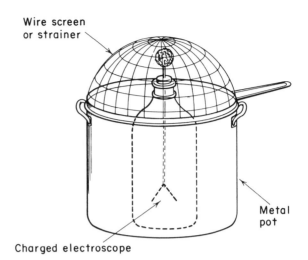

Wire screen or strainer

Metal pot

Charged electroscope

The Leyden Jar

Materials you will need:

1. *Thin drinking glass or plastic tumbler*
2. *Aluminum or tin foil (sufficient to cover the inside and outside of the glass or tumbler)*
3. *Plastic comb*
4. *Ten paper clips*
5. *The electrophorus built in an earlier experiment*

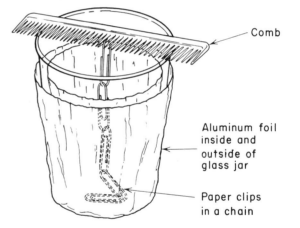

Comb

Aluminum foil inside and outside of glass jar

Paper clips in a chain

IN the year 1745 the Dutch mathematician and scientist Pieter van Musschenbroek, experimenting at the University of Leyden in Holland, lined a thin glass jar inside and out with metal foil and inserted a brass rod with a knob at the top through a cover. Contact with the inner foil was achieved by means of a chain. Musschenbroek found out that he could use this new device to store electrical charges.

This was a very important discovery because before his time, though different ways had been found of producing electrical charges by friction, no method had been found for storing them. Musschenbroek's discovery was named the Leyden jar after the town in Hol-

land in which the experiments were conducted. We can now build a simple Leyden jar and duplicate the results that were obtained by early experimenters over 200 years ago.

Wrap aluminum or tin foil on the inside and outside of a glass to about three-quarters of the way up from the bottom. The foil must be pressed tightly against the bottom and the sides so that the only separation between the inside and the outside foils is the glass itself. Make a chain out of paper clips by looping one into the other. Push the top one through a comb so that it will stay in place. Use enough clips so that the bottom one touches the inside foil. You have finished your modern version of the Leyden jar. Now let us use it.

To put a charge into the Leyden jar, use the electrophorus built earlier. (Other ways of charging it require the use of high voltage generating machines). Bring the charged disk of the electrophorus near the clip in the comb. A spark jumps to the clip. Do this a number of times. After a quantity of such charges have been put into the Leyden jar, connect a short piece of wire from the outer foil to the clip. You should now get a rather powerful spark, much greater than that which you are able to draw from the electrophorus.

Here is why: Every time the disk was discharged into the Leyden jar, that charge was stored in the jar, and after several such successive charges, we accumulated quite a substantial charge. This is very much like filling a glass with a teaspoon and then spilling it all at once.

The Leyden jar can also be discharged with your bare hands by touching the outer foil and the clip at the same time. You may get quite a shock, so be careful and be sure the glass is standing on a table when you try this.

The ability of the Leyden jar to hold its charge depends to a great extent on the quality of the glass we use. If you are not successful with the first or second glass or tumbler, try a small beaker of the kind used in chemical experiments. It is made of a type of "hard" glass which is very suitable for this experiment.

You can also try the following. As you charge the Leyden jar, hold the outer foil with your hand. This will allow the jar to take on a greater charge. If you would like to compare the total charge obtained when you hold the outside of the glass with the charge you get with the glass resting on the table, note the intensity and length of the spark after an equal number of charges.

If there is any doubt in your mind that a Leyden jar can store great charges, be reminded that Benjamin Franklin used the charge from one of them to kill a large turkey. Another early experiment with Leyden jars involved a circle of monks who joined hands. When the first and the last monk made contact with a charged Leyden jar 6 feet high, they all received quite a nice shock. According to the monastic chronicler of this event "to a man they leaped several feet into the air."

The Leyden jar was the forerunner of the modern-day capacitor, an important component used to store electrical charges. Many different capacitors of various constructions and characteristics are used today. They function on the same principle as does the Leyden jar. The design is much refined, and new techniques of construction have evolved rapidly, but every capacitor uses essentially two conductors, which correspond to the inside and outside foil of our Leyden jar. They are separated by a dielectric or nonconductor, which takes the place of the glass jar.

18 Building a Proof Plane

Materials you will need:

1. *Glass rod of any suitable length*
2. *Small metal disk about the size of a penny (a penny can also be used)*
3. *Some modeling cement (or any other quick-drying glue), modeling clay, or sealing wax to affix the metal to the rod*

WE may sometimes encounter static charges which are so high that if we were to bring them near the electroscope, they would damage our instrument. At another time, we may wish to measure a charge but cannot conveniently bring the charged object and the electroscope together. In either of these cases it may be best to use a proof plane to bring a small charge to the electroscope. This device is very easily constructed. Just affix a small metal disk, the size of a penny (a penny can also be used), to a glass rod or glass tube. The metal disk can be cemented to the rod with quick-drying cement, modeling clay, or held with a few drops of hot sealing wax.

To use the proof plane, hold it by the glass rod, and touch the electrified body with the metal disk. A small charge will flow onto the proof plane from the electrified body when the disk is withdrawn. This small charge can now be brought to the electroscope and transferred to it, either by contact or induction.

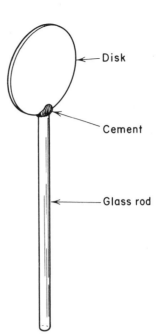

Experiment with Charged Grains

Materials you will need:

1. *Wire clothes hanger*
2. *Two grains of puffed rice (you can also use puffed wheat or two little balls made of cotton)*
3. *Light tin foil (from chewing gum or candy wrapper) just large enough to cover the puffed rice*
4. *Two feet of thin silk or nylon thread*
5. *Comb and some wool or nylon*
6. *Glass rod and some silk*

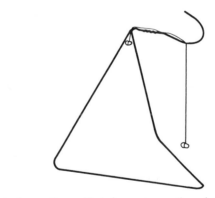

How to hang the puffed rice grains on the wire stand so that only one is used and the other is safely out of the way.

Figure A

BEND a wire clothes hanger into the shape shown in the illustrations. This gives us a convenient little stand for a number of interesting experiments to follow. We will also need some little light objects which can best be made from puffed rice. Tie one grain of puffed rice to each end of a 16-inch length of thin silk or nylon thread. Now cover each grain with a little piece of light tin foil. (This can be obtained from a chewing gum wrapper soaked in

warm water to separate the paper from the foil.) For the moment we will use only one of these grains, so hang one over the hook on the hanger and put the other out of the way as illustrated in Figure A. That is all for the preparation; now for the experiments.

1. Rub a comb with a piece of wool or nylon. This moves the electrons from the wool to the comb and places a negative charge on

the comb. Touch the grain hanging on the thread with the comb. The grain will immediately take on a charge and fly off as shown in Figure B. No matter how hard you try, you cannot make it touch the charged comb again until you touch it first with your fingers to remove its charge. You can now bring the comb up again and repeat the experiment. Bring the wool you used for rubbing the comb near the charged grain. There will be attraction.

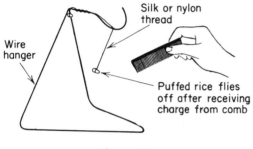

Figure B

2. Repeat the experiment using a glass rod or tumbler rubbed with silk. This removes some electrons from the glass to the silk and leaves a positive charge on the glass. Touch the grain with the rod. It will take on a charge, fly off, and won't approach the glass rod again until the charges are removed with your hand or dissipate into the air. Bring the silk used to rub the rod near the grain, and they will attract each other.

3. Charge the grain from the comb again, but this time bring the charged glass rod near it. See how the grain flies over to the rod? Then charge the grain from the rod, and bring the charged comb nearby. Again there is attraction between them. We can therefore make the general and most important statement that objects with like charges repel and those with unlike charges attract.

4. Hang both grains of puffed rice evenly over the hanger so that they touch each other. Bring the charged comb near and touch them. In a moment they will acquire a charge and fly away as shown in Figure C. Take the comb away, and you will see that the two little grains will stand apart from each other. They both have acquired the same charge and repel each

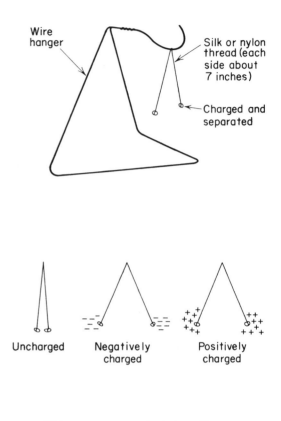

Charges are concentrated on the far sides, on the surfaces.

Figure C

other. Touch one of the grains with your fingers to remove its charge. It will then be attracted by the other grain that is still charged and take on half of its charge. They will repel again, but this time the separation will not be quite as great because the charges on each grain are not as strong. Repeat the experiment with the charged glass rod, and also try it with other charged objects.

5. Our little grains can also be used to determine the polarity of an unknown charge. Here's how: Put a charge on one of the grains, using either the comb for a negative charge or the glass rod for a positive one. Approach the charged grain with the object whose charge you wish to determine. If there is repulsion, the charges are the same. If there is attraction, the charges are opposite.

The Swinging Grain

Materials you will need:

1. *Two rubber balloons*
2. *Wire hanger stand (from the previous experiment)*
3. *Grain of foil-covered puffed rice on silk or nylon thread (from the previous experiment)*
4. *Some wool or fur*
5. *Piece of Saran wrap*

RUB one of the balloons with the wool (or fur or nylon) to give it a negative charge, and rub the other balloon with the Saran wrap to give it a positive charge.

Holding one balloon in each hand, approach the single grain of puffed rice from both sides. It will be attracted to one of the balloons (which one doesn't matter), touch it, and pick up some of the charge there by contact (Figure A). Now that it has the same charge as the balloon it has touched, it will be repelled. Since its charge is opposite to that of the other balloon, it will be attracted to it. Once it touches there, the puffed rice will give up its charge and pick up the charge of the balloon it now touches. It will be repelled, go back to the first balloon, and the cycle repeats.

During each trip, our little grain of puffed rice reduces the total charge on each balloon

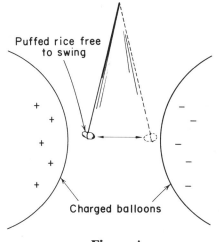

Figure A

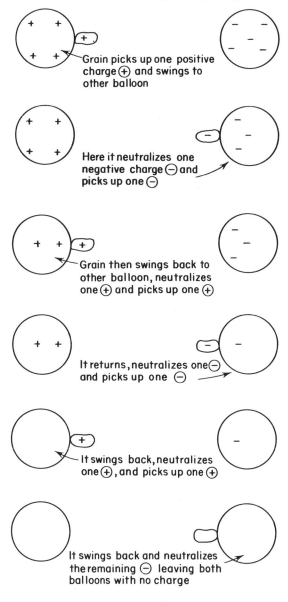

Assume attraction is first to positively charged balloon

Grain picks up one positive charge ⊕ and swings to other balloon

Here it neutralizes one negative charge ⊖ and picks up one ⊖

Grain then swings back to other balloon, neutralizes one ⊕ and picks up one ⊕

It returns, neutralizes one ⊖ and picks up one ⊖

It swings back, neutralizes one ⊕, and picks up one ⊕

It swings back and neutralizes the remaining ⊖ leaving both balloons with no charge

Figure B

by bringing a few electrons from the negatively charged to the positively charged (electron hungry) balloon. Eventually the charges on both balloons will become neutralized, and the trips back and forth will come to an end. This is a rather amusing experiment. Nonetheless, be sure that you understand fully why the grain acts the way it does (Figure B).

[23]

Making a Static Electricity Pendulum

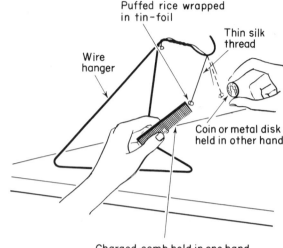

Puffed rice wrapped in tin-foil

Thin silk thread

Wire hanger

Coin or metal disk held in other hand

Charged comb held in one hand

Materials you will need:

1. *Wire hanger stand (from previous experiments)*
2. *Foil-covered puffed rice (from previous experiments)*
3. *Comb and some wool or fur*
4. *Coin or other piece of metal the size of a quarter or larger*

FOR this experiment we will use the wire frame which we built for an earlier experiment. Hang one of the grains, so that it is free to swing as shown in the illustration. We are now ready to make a little electrostatic pendulum.

Rub the comb briskly with the wool so that it attains a good charge. Hold the charged comb in one hand and a large coin in the other. When you approach the little grain of puffed rice with the comb, you will see that the grain will be attracted to it. As soon as it touches the comb, it will receive a charge, and since like charges repel, it will fly off in the direction of the coin and hit it (if you are holding the coin properly). The charge will then be transferred to the coin, leaving the grain uncharged. The grain will then be attracted to the comb, be charged again, and the whole process will repeat itself very much like the action of a pendulum.

An interesting variation of this experiment requires a glass rod and a piece of silk in addition to the comb and the wool. Charge both the comb and the glass rod by rubbing the first with the wool and the second with the silk. Hold them on opposite sides of the puffed rice hanging by the thread. The puffed rice will be attracted to either the glass rod or the comb and be charged there. Assuming that it has touched the comb, it will have received a negative charge and will be attracted to the positively charged glass rod. There it will receive a positive charge and be attracted to the comb again. Back and forth it will go in this fashion for a really lively action.

Benjamin Franklin used a device based on this very principle to announce the passing of lightning clouds over his home. He used an electric charge from the clouds to charge a small clapper, which then was made to swing between two little bells. The ringing of the bells announced the presence of lightning clouds over his house.

Making a Paper Spider

Materials you will need:

1. *Small piece of newspaper*
2. *Scissors*
3. *Piece of polyethylene*

FOR this experiment you will need a small piece of newspaper measuring about 3 by 5 inches. Cut eight narrow strips down the length of the 5-inch side to a depth of about 3 inches as shown in Figure A. These eight

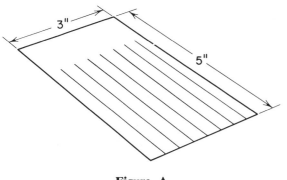

Figure A

long, narrow strips are the legs of our spider, and the remaining uncut part is the body.

Hold the spider against the wall, with its legs down, and rub it with the polyethylene for about ten strokes in a downward direction. You will note that after only a few strokes the spider will stick to the wall. Holding the spider by the "body," lift it from the wall. See what happens? The legs spread apart and move around (Figure B). Some will even reach up towards your hand.

What happened is this: The paper spider

acquired a charge from the polyethylene. Since each of the legs has the same charge, they repel one another and try to get as far apart as possible. We showed this effect previously with the two long strips of newspaper.

While you hold the spider body up with one hand, put a finger between the legs. Note how they jump onto your finger and cling to it until all the charges have leaked off, leaving the legs limp. To repeat the experiment, simply hold the spider onto the wall and rub again .

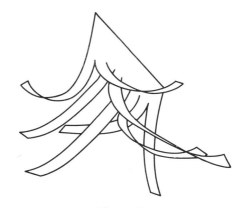

Figure B

An Electrostatic Palm Tree

23

Materials you will need:

1. *Stiff piece of wire or a wire hanger about 1 foot long*
2. *Piece of tissue paper large enough for eight strips ¼ inch wide and about 10 inches long*
3. *Insulating handle of plastic or glass*
4. *Charged balloon or electro-phorus*

IF you thought the spider was fun, this electrostatic tree will really demonstrate the repelling effect that equally charged strips of paper have on each other.

Bend a thick piece of wire, about 20 inches long, at each end to form two loops. Now cut eight strips of tissue paper, each of them ¼ inch wide and 10 inches long. Push these strips through one of the loops so that they project for a distance of 5 inches on either side. Squeeze the sides of the loop together to hold the strips in place. To make our "tree," we must now apply an electrostatic charge to the strips. We can get this charge either from a charged balloon or from the charge-carrying disk of an electrophorus.

Before applying either, however, we must attach our tree to an insulating handle, which can be a glass rod or a plastic rod held to the

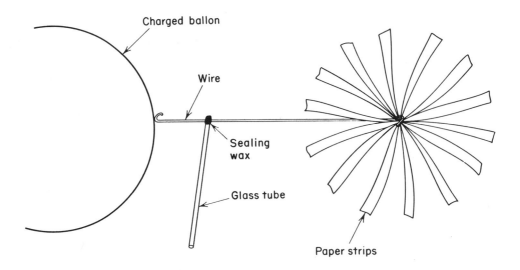

Charged balloon

Wire

Sealing wax

Glass tube

Paper strips

wire with quick-drying cement or sealing wax. It may be advisable to wrap the wire around the insulating handle to be sure that the two parts hold together properly. You might also use cellophane tape or modeling clay rather than glue or sealing wax to hold the wire to the handle.

Now charge your balloon (by rubbing it with wool or fur or nylon) or your electrophorus (see Experiment 15). When you have a good charge on it, hold the palm tree by its handle and touch the lower loop to the charged point on the balloon or electrophorus disk. You will see that the crown of the tree will spread out just like a living palm. By so doing, it indicates the presence of static electricity.

Making a Simple Electrostatic Charge Detector

Materials you will need:
1. *Cork*
2. *Sewing needle*
3. *Small piece of lightweight paper*
4. *Little bit of glue or scotch tape*

THE purpose of the charge detector is to indicate the presence of electrostatic charges. We can make this very simple and yet surprisingly sensitive instrument in just a few minutes.

Cut out a rectangular piece of paper about 1 inch wide and 2 inches long. Fold this paper in half lengthwise. Then bring its two ends together lightly so as to find the center, and cut off the inside corner. When you open the paper again, you will have a centrally located V-shaped opening, as shown in the illustration. Now cut out another smaller strip of paper ¼ inch wide and 1½ inches long and paste it on the previously prepared paper at the center so that the small strip extends ¼ inch above the opening. This arrangement is very clearly shown in the illustration. (If you do not have any glue, the little strip of paper may also be held with a small piece of scotch tape, or in an emergency, even with staples.)

Make a lengthwise hole in the center of the cork with the sewing needle. Then reverse

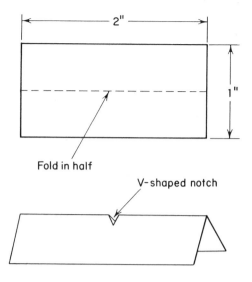

Fold in half

V-shaped notch

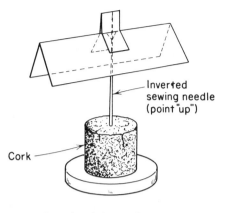

Inverted sewing needle (point "up")

Cork

Completed charge detector

the needle, and insert it again so that its pointed end sticks upward out of the cork. Now take the previously prepared paper and balance it at its center on the point of the needle so that it can very easily rotate. Be careful not to pierce the paper.

To test the detector, rub a comb, a glass rod, a fountain pen, a toothbrush, a straw, or even another piece of paper with wool, silk, nylon, or anything else you happen to have around, and bring any of the objects that you have rubbed *near* the charge detector (without touching it.) You will see that it will immediately turn and point in the direction of the charged object.

You can establish the sensitivity of our

little detector in any one of many different ways. Rub the object just a little bit, and determine the least amount of friction it takes to get an indication of charge. Also, see how far from the detector the charged object can be held and still give a definite indication of charge.

The electrostatic charge indicator works on the principle of the attraction of a neutral body (the charge detector) to a charged body. It does not indicate whether the attraction is to a positively or to a negatively charged object. Nonetheless, you will find this an amazingly sensitive device. If you wish to identify the polarity of the charges (whether they are positive or negative), you will have to use the electroscope shown in Experiment 12.

An Electrostatic Merry-go-round

Materials you will need:

1. *Charge detector built in the previous experiment*
2. *Glass or a jar which fits over the charge detector*
3. *Piece of polyethylene*

PLACE the charge detector built in the previous experiment on a table, and put the glass or jar (be sure it is dry) over it so that the paper indicator is free to rotate within the enclosing glass. Here is a chance to challenge anyone to make the charge detector turn in any predetermined direction without removing the glass. This feat may sound impossible, but it is really very simple once you know something about static electricity.

Here is how to do it: Hold the glass with one hand. With the polyethylene in the other hand, rub that side of the glass toward which you want your charge detector to turn. (If polyethylene is not available, a piece of silk or cotton will also do the job very nicely). After a few strokes, the charge detector will indeed turn and point at the very spot at which you are rubbing. If you want to move it in a different direction, rub at another point around the outer surface of the glass, and the charge detector will soon turn in that direction. If you are very skillful, you should be able to rub the glass in the same direction all around, and the detector will follow your hand as you rub around the glass. You now have an electrostatic merry-go-round.

There is another way in which you can cause your charge director to change direction, and you can do this without even touching the glass with your hand or anything else, difficult as that may seem. Merely bring any electrostatically charged object (such as a fountain pen, a plastic rod, a toothbrush, a balloon, etc.) near the glass and you will see the charge detector point directly at the charged object (see earlier experiments on how to put a charge on an object). Rubbing your feet on a rug may even give you sufficient charge to have the

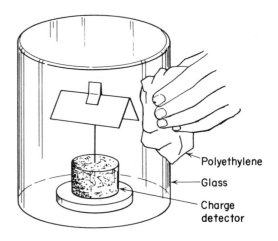

Polyethylene
Glass
Charge detector

charge detector follow your finger as you move it around the glass.

Here is what is happening: When you rubbed the glass in the first experiment, you put a positive electrostatic charge on a certain area of the glass, and this caused the neutral charge detector to be attracted to that area. In this new experiment, you place a charge on the inside of the glass by induction. When the charged object is brought near the glass, it repels like charges from the outside to the inside of the glass, and those charges which find themselves on the inside of the glass attract the neutral charge detector. The experiment will work whether the charge on the object is positive or negative. You can try this by first using a charged object and then using that material which was used to charge it.

26   The Free-wheeling Straw

Materials you will need:

1. *Bottle with a cork*
2. *Straw*
3. *Thin silk thread*
4. *Thumbtack*

THIS simplified version of the foregoing experiment will show how a straw suspended inside a bottle can be made to move without touching either the bottle or the straw.

Here is how: Cut off a piece of straw measuring less than the width of the bottle you use. Tie the silk thread tightly around its center, and hold the other end of the thread to the cork by means of the thumbtack. Set a perfectly dry bottle (leave it open in a warm place for a few hours) on a table. Drop the straw in, and make sure that it is free to rotate. Put the cork in the bottle. You are all set.

After the straw settles down in a horizontal position, rub your feet on the rug, point your finger at the straw, and it will turn to you. The straw will also follow any other charged object. This experiment makes quite a neat party trick.

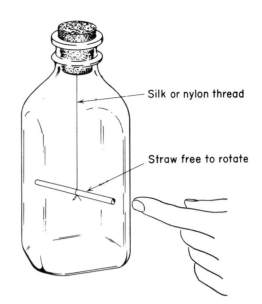

Silk or nylon thread

Straw free to rotate

The Magic Finger

27

Materials you will need:

1. Wooden pencil

HERE is an interesting little party stunt that requires no preparation. Balance a wooden pencil on the back of a chair so that it is free to move and challenge anyone to move the pencil in any desired direction or make it fall down without (1) touching it, (2) blowing on it, or (3) causing the chair to move.

When everyone gives up, you simply shuffle your feet on a rug and hold a finger near the tip of the pencil. You will see that the uncharged pencil will follow your finger. The reason is that the pencil is attracted by the charge you have put on yourself by the friction between your feet and the rug.

The same control over the pencil can also be exerted by any other charged object, such as a pen or cocktail mixer rubbed with wool, silk, fur, or nylon.

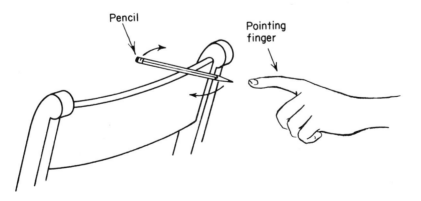

Pencil

Pointing finger

Electrostatic "Jumping Beans"

Materials you will need:

1. *Plastic box (not deeper than 1 inch)*
2. *Some small, light objects such as puffed rice, saw dust, tiny bits of cork, small pieces of paper, or tiny balls of cotton*
3. *Piece of aluminum or tin foil to line the bottom of the plastic box*
4. *Piece of nylon or wool*

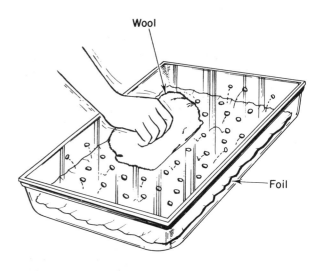

LINE the bottom of the plastic box with the aluminum foil, and then put some of the light material that you have available (such as puffed rice) into the box and close the cover as shown . With the wool or nylon rub the cover of the box vigorously, and watch what happens. The material will fly up to the cover, stay there for a brief period, and then fly off again, and so forth. If you rub briskly enough, and the weather is in your favor, this up and down jumping will continue even after you have stopped rubbing.

If you really want to have some fun, wrap up a dozen small pieces of cork or puffed rice, individually, with small pieces of tin foil. These will provide you with light but conductive little objects. Place them in the box and rub the cover. You will be surprised and delighted by the results.

Here is what happens: By rubbing the cover we put a negative charge on it. When the charge becomes strong enough, it attracts the light, uncharged objects. As soon as they strike the cover, they also become charged and are repelled. When they fall down onto the tin foil, they discharge and are ready for the next trip. Thus we have a continuous process which consists of attraction, charging, repulsion, discharging, attraction again, and so forth. If you use the foil covered pieces of puffed rice, they will all jump up and down wildly. If you use some other material, some of the

objects may stick to the cover and not be repelled. In order to get them off, you simply stop rubbing and touch the cover above the point where this little object is located with your finger. You will see that the particle will immediately fly off.

The attraction of light objects towards grounded objects by means of high electrostatic charges is utilized in industry to do some amazing jobs. Here are some good examples: paint particles are often given a high potential charge (about 100,000 volts) as they are discharged from a spray gun. Directed towards a grounded object, the charged paint is attracted to it and will cover it thoroughly, not only on the front but also on the top, bottom, both sides, and back .

Sandpaper is made by similarly directing charged abrasive particles onto adhesive-coated paper. The grains stand on edge as did our puffed rice particles, thus giving a longer-wearing and faster-cutting sandpaper than could be produced otherwise. Imitation velvet and suede are also produced by a similar process. The process is generally known as electrostatic coating.

A Hair-Raising Experiment

Materials you will need:

1. *Comb*
2. *Head with dry hair*

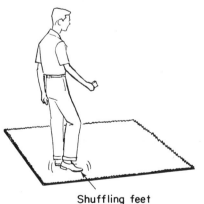

Charged comb

HAVE you ever noticed some crackling when you combed your hair on a cool, dry winter day and also that your hair seemed to "stand up"? You were actually generating very high electrostatic charges. What happens is that the comb removes electrons from your hair and acquires a high negative charge, whereas the hair, having lost electrons, becomes positively charged. If you comb your dry hair in front of a mirror on a dry day in a dark room, you will actually see many tiny sparks jumping from the comb to the hair.

After you have combed your hair briskly, hold the comb about ¼ inch from a water tap. You will see a tiny charge jump from the comb to the tap, and you will also be able to hear it. Believe it or not, if the spark is about ⅛ inch long, you will have generated a charge of about 5,000 volts!

Plaster Your Wall with Cards

Materials you will need:

1. *Some playing cards*

ON any cool, dry day you can stick playing cards to a wall without using any glue. Hold the cards in your hand, and rub your feet on a dry carpet. As you approach the wall,

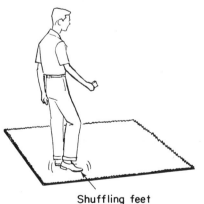

Shuffling feet on rug

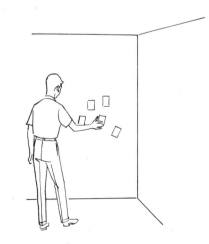

quickly slap a card up against it. The card should stick to the wall. The charge you acquired by rubbing your feet on the rug will have been transferred to the cards, and being charged, they will readily stick to the neutral surface. This process can be repeated over and over again, and you can put cards all over the wall without doing any damage.

If you have no rug, you can make the cards stick by first rubbing them against your clothing and then slamming them up against the wall. This technique may sometimes work better than the rug method.

A card will stay on the wall for quite some time, oftentimes for days, depending mostly on the weather and the charge on the card.

31 Picking up Salt Electrostatically

Materials you will need:

1. *Some salt*
2. *Pocket comb*
3. *Some wool (or fur)*

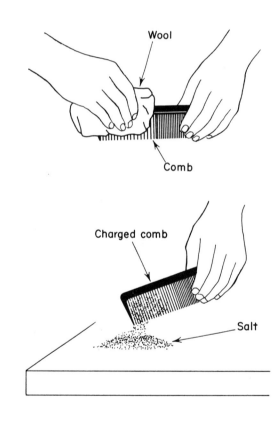
Wool
Comb
Charged comb
Salt

SPILL a little salt on a table or tablecloth and challenge anyone to pick up the salt without touching either the table or the tablecloth. This may sound impossible, but it is really quite simple.

Rub the comb with the wool (or run it through your hair if your hair is dry) to put a charge on it. Then bring the comb near the salt, and immediately the grains will jump up to the comb. A few grains will fly off again as soon as they have acquired the charge from the comb, but most of them will stick. Rub off the salt which sticks to the comb, recharge it with the wool, and you can then go back to pick up the remaining salt.

For variety, you can sprinkle a little fine pepper on top of the salt and again defy anyone to separate the pepper from the salt. You can do it by passing the charged comb about an inch or so above the mixture of the pepper and the salt. Since the lighter bits of pepper are more easily attracted, they will jump to the comb, leaving the salt behind. You may have to repeat the experiment several times to be sure all the pepper is removed.

If you wish, you can try this experiment with other powdered materials, such as flour or sugar.

The Hindu Thread Trick

> **Materials you will need:**
>
> 1. *About a foot of cotton thread and a foot of nylon or silk thread*
> 2. *Plastic comb*
> 3. *Piece of wool*

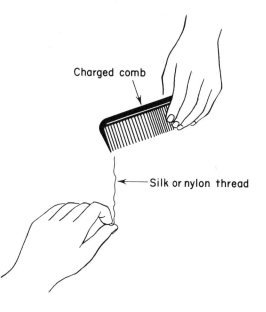

Charged comb

Silk or nylon thread

HERE is a modern version of the famous Hindu rope trick (in miniature). Rub the pocket comb brisky with the wool to give the comb a strong charge. Hold onto the comb, and then put away the wool. Now take the cotton thread in the free hand so that about 6 inches of thread are left hanging loose. Bring the comb near the free end of the thread so that it touches the comb. Draw the comb up and away slowly so that the thread finally becomes separated from the comb. If the weather is with you, you will find that you can make the thread stand upright even after it is about a half inch away from the comb. Move the comb all around, and the thread will follow it faithfully. (This will take a little practice.)

Try the same experiment with the nylon thread and notice the difference. You can also try it with the threads lying on a table. The ends will weave about like snakes being "charmed" by music as the comb is moved all around them.

Dancing Soap Bubbles

> **Materials you will need:**
>
> 1. *Pocket comb*
> 2. *Piece of wool or fur*
> 3. *Means of producing soap bubbles*

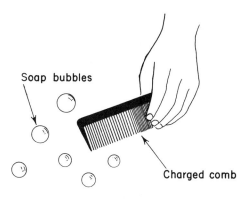

Soap bubbles

Charged comb

CHARGE the comb by rubbing it briskly with the wool or fur. Then blow a few bubbles. As they begin to fall bring the comb nearby, and you will see that they are attracted to it. If you quickly remove the comb just before the bubbles touch it and burst, you can control them very nicely. With a little practice you can even make them do a "dance."

Set up a bubble on a fixed surface such as a soft cloth or even the pipe used to blow it. Bring the charged comb near, and the bubble will be attracted and become distorted. It will almost take on the shape of an egg. If the attraction is strong enough, the bubble may even be drawn away from where it sits and fly right onto the comb.

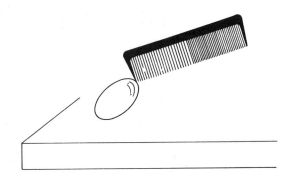

The Charged Tape

Materials you will need:
1. Roll of friction tape

TAKE a roll of friction tape (the kind used to insulate electrical wiring) into a completely dark room, and give your eyes a chance to get used to the dark. Then quickly pull off a piece of friction tape. As you do this, look at that place on the roll where the tape separates. You will see a bluish glow there as long as you unroll the tape.

The glow is actually a great number of

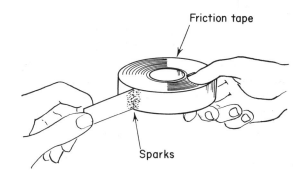

very tiny sparks (caused by static electricity) that jump from the roll to the strip of tape as it is being unwound.

Surprise The Cat

Materials you will need:
1. A live cat

ON a cool and clear winter day, stroke a cat fairly rapidly with the hand. You will see that its fur will stand up towards the hand, and at the same time a faint, crackling noise will be heard. This crackling is caused by tiny sparks which jump between the cat and the hand. You can even see the sparks if this experiment is performed in a dark room.

After having stroked the cat for a while, bring your knuckle close to its nose. The

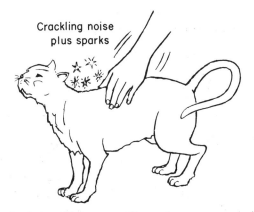

spark that will jump will surely come as quite a surprise.

Cleaning Your Records Electrostatically

Saran wrap

Record

Materials you will need:

1. Piece of Saran wrap

IF your records are dusty, you can clean them easily without touching the record surfaces and the delicate grooves. Here's how. Rub a piece of Saran wrap against some silk or cotton. Then crumple it, and hold it about an inch over the revolving record. The strongly charged Saran will attract and hold the dust from the spinning record. Start at the outside, and move the Saran over the entire record surface to be sure the whole record is cleaned.

If you watch very closely, you should actually be able to see the uncharged dust particles jump from the surface of the record to the Saran wrap. One piece can clean several records. When finished, discard the Saran wrap.

Rub for Your Light

Materials you will need:

1. Fluorescent tube (a burnt-out one will serve)
2. Polyethylene bag or Saran wrap

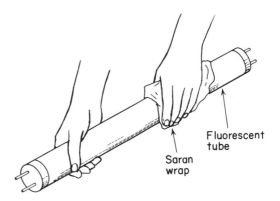

Fluorescent tube

Saran wrap

YOU can make a fluorescent tube glow without connecting it to anything simply by rubbing its surface with Saran wrap, a polyethylene bag, or a piece of fur or wool.

This experiment is best conducted in a room that is as dark as possible because the light we will produce will not be very bright. Hold the tube in one hand, and rub it lightly but rapidly with the chosen material held in the other hand. After a few seconds, the tube will give off light in the areas where it is being rubbed. The faster you rub, the more light you will get. Also try this experiment with other rubbing materials, and see which one gives the best results.

Here is why we get our light. The fluorescent tube is filled with mercury vapor, and the inner surface of the glass is coated with a white material called a phosphor. This phosphor gives off light whenever it is struck by ultraviolet rays. As we rub the lamp, we remove some electrons from the glass, giving it a positive charge and causing an electron movement inside the tube. As the electrons "shoot" through the tube, they collide with atoms of mercury vapor and produce ultra-violet rays. These in turn strike the phosphor coating, and thus light is given off.

A new type of lighting called "electro-luminescent lighting" has recently been made available. It consist of glowing panels instead of incandescent bulbs or fluorescent tubes and has very much in common with the light that we produce by rubbing the fluorescent tube.

How to Charge Your Friends to 10,000 Volts

Materials you will need:

1. *Four strong glasses or jars*
2. *Piece of fur (a fur collar or muff will do)*
3. *Board or large book*
4. *A friend*

WITHOUT the slightest danger, you can charge someone to a potential of thousands of volts and then discharge him by drawing large sparks from his fingers. Let us try it.

Before we build our charges, we must be sure we won't lose them right away, so we have to insulate the person being charged. We accomplish this by means of an insulation platform, for which we need four glasses and a board.

Place the glasses, which must be absolutely dry, on the floor near a radiator or a water tap, and separate them sufficiently so that you can place the board on top and thus construct a stable and safe platform.

Have the person to be charged stand on that platform. Be sure that no part of his body

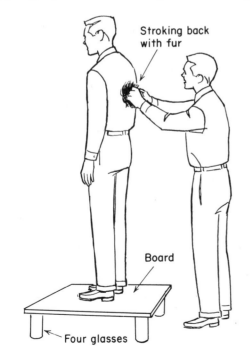

Stroking back with fur

Board

Four glasses

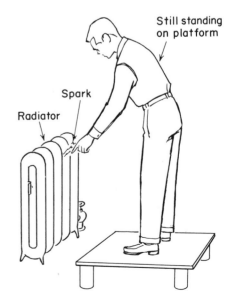

Still standing on platform

Spark

Radiator

touches anything. Now stroke his back vigorously with a piece of fur for about a minute, and then let him bring his finger near the radiator or the tap. You will see that quite a spark jumps across. The charged person can also touch someone else who is not insulated from the floor and create a nice spark in this way as well.

What you have done is to build up a strong electrostatic charge by rubbing with the fur. This charge may be as high as 10,000 volts or even more. As a further experiment, try rubbing with wool, nylon, rubber, polyethylene, or any other material, and see which gives you the greater charge as indicated by the length of the spark you can draw.

You might also try several layers of polyethylene to stand on for insulation, instead of the glasses and the board.

The Triboelectric or Electrostatic Series

Now you are on your own. You can experiment to your heart's content in static electricity, and as a guide you can refer to the triboelectric series (also known as the electrostatic series) which is presented here in tabular form.

As far back as 1757, J. C. Wilcke noted that various substances, such as glass, silk, wool, and amber, could be arranged in a triboelectric series. He showed that as you rub any two different materials together, they will become electrified and develop opposite charges. The one higher up on the list will give up electrons and thus become positively charged. The one below will have gained those electrons and thus acquire a negative charge.

The farther apart the materials are on the list, the easier it is to work with them and the higher the charge will be. You can determine the presence and nature of the charge by means of the charge detector or electroscope. The exact charge on each body depends on its molecular structure as well as the condition of its surface.

Positive Polarity $(+)$
  Asbestos
  Rabbit's fur
  Glass
  Mica
  Nylon
  Wool
  Cat's fur
  Silk
  Paper
  Cotton
  Wood
  Lucite
  Sealing wax
  Amber
  Polystyrene
  Polyethylene
  Rubber balloon
  Sulphur
  Celluloid
  Hard rubber
  Vinylite
  Saran wrap
Negative Polarity $(-)$

magnetism

Early History of Magnetism

The ancient Greeks discovered that certain stones found near the city of Magnesia in Asia Minor had the power to attract bits of iron. Quite appropriately they called these stones *magnetite*. Legend also tells us of a shepherd boy named Magnes, who thrust his iron staff into a hole containing magnetite and found to his dismay that he was unable to remove it. Another story dating back about 2,300 years tells of Ptolemy Philadelphos who had the entire dome of a temple at Alexandria made of magnetite, so that he might be able to suspend a statue in mid-air. The experiment was a failure. Today, it is known that magnetite is an iron ore (a chemical compound of the metal, iron, and the gas, oxygen) which possesses magnetic qualities. It is an unrefined product of nature and is found in nearly all parts of the world. Magnetite is also called *loadstone* or *lodestone*. This name came about from its earliest use, its ability to "lead" in a certain direction.

The first legendary account of the use of the magnet for giving directions dates back to 2637 B.C. Hoang-ti, who was said to have founded the Chinese Empire and reigned for 100 years, was pursuing the rebellious prince Tchiyeou and got lost in a dense fog that rolled in from the broad plains. In danger of losing sight of the prince, Hoang-ti constructed a chariot upon which he mounted a female figure that always pointed towards the south, no matter which way the chariot was driven. With the aid of this primitive compass he was able to follow and capture the rebellious prince.

For many of the experiments in this section, a permanent magnet will be required.

Generally available steel magnets are shaped either like a straight bar or like the letter "U". The latter is sometimes called a horseshoe magnet and is usually stronger because the air gap between the poles is smaller. Both types are illustrated, and they are essentially interchangeable in any experiment.

Magnets made out of alnico (aluminum, nickel, and cobalt) are much more powerful than steel magnets and are used in almost all loudspeakers manufactured today. Frequently, discarded loudspeakers are available from local radio service shops. Their magnets are round, usually about 1 inch in diameter and 1 inch high, and they are excellent for our experiments. If a magnet is to be purchased, it will be well worth the difference in price to get an alnico magnet.

If unobtainable elsewhere, serviceable alnico magnets can be secured from such things as magnetic pot holders, magnetic pencils, magnetic toys, or containers used for the purpose of hiding keys (the latter item is obtainable in most hardware stores). Very cheap variety store horseshoe magnets are usually not suited for these experiments because they are weak to begin with and also lose their magnetism very rapidly.

There are three kinds of magnets: the lodestone (magnetite), which is a natural magnet; (2) the permanent magnet, which is an artificial magnet and will be used in this section; (3) the electromagnet, which is a temporary, artificial magnet and will be dealt with in the next section.

How to Read Your Compass

> **Materials you will need:**
>
> *1. Compass (a 10 cent compass from a variety store will do)*

IN many of our experiments we will need the help of a compass. This handy little device was not originally developed for experimental purposes, but rather, as we all know, as a very important navigational aid. Let us find out how a compass is used.

Looking at one, you will see that a compass is round and marked with at least the four letters N, E, S, and W, which stand for North, East, South, and West. There may be perhaps four more markings which use a combination of these four letters, such as NE, SE, SW, and NW, standing for Northeast, Southeast, Southwest, and Northwest. They indicate, as you will note, a position between the two directions whose letters are used. For example, NE indicates a position exactly halfway between North (N) and East (E).

You will also see that in the center of the compass is a supported needle which is free to turn when the compass is held in a horizontal direction. This little needle will either have one end blue and the other end uncolored or have an arrow at one end.

To use the compass, lay it flat on the table. The needle will come to rest after a few seconds and will point in a particular direction. Turn the compass housing so that the blue end or the arrow of the needle lines itself up exactly with the N marked on the compass. That is all that there is to using a compass. You will note that as you turned the compass, the needle itself stayed in place pointing in the same direction, with the arrow or blue end *always pointing North*. Now that the compass is set up, you can tell at a glance which way is East, West, North, or South by just looking at

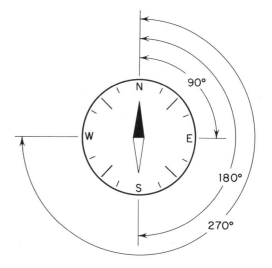

the markings on the compass. If you look straight down at the compass and North happens to be ahead of you, East will be on your right, West on the left, and South behind you.

The compass is also marked in numbers starting from 0 at N, going all the way around in a clockwise direction to 360, which will again be at N. These numbers indicate degrees. They tell how many degrees away we are from North, so that

> East is 90 degrees from North
> South is 180 degrees from North
> West is 270 degrees from North

It is important that you know how to use a compass, because in one of our experiments, we will have to determine which is the North-South direction so that we can magnetize a rod using the earth's magnetic field.

[41]

What Will a Magnet Attract?

Materials you will need:

1.   Magnet
2.   Number of objects to be tested (see text)

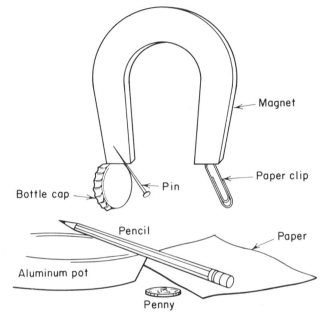

A magnet, we have learned, is an object that has the ability to attract iron and other magnetic materials. The pull of the magnet is called magnetism. This is an invisible force which can be noticed only by the effect it produces. When a material becomes magnetized, it doesn't change its weight, size, or appearance, so that we cannot tell by looking, weighing, or measuring whether we have a magnet or not. Neither can magnetism be smelled, tasted, heard, or felt. To prove this, hold a magnet next to your ear and listen, then try to smell it or taste it, and you will see that in no way can you tell that you are in fact dealing with a magnet.

Let us find out what materials are attracted by a magnet. Assemble a number of items such as paper clips, pins, nails, a drinking glass, a piece of paper, an aluminum pot, a tin can, some needles, coins, a rubber band, a piece of wood, a strip of cardboard, a wooden pencil, something made of plastic, and any other thing which you would like to test.

Bring the magnet close to every one of these objects, one at a time, and separate them according to which is attracted and which is not attracted by the magnet. If you are careful in your observation, you will find that only materials containing iron, steel, cobalt, or nickel (singly, or in combination) are attracted to a greater or lesser degree by the magnet. All the others are not. If the magnet is a strong one and the objects are small or light, they will even jump up to it. A so-called "tin can" will be strongly attracted to the magnet due to the fact that we really do not have a can which is made of tin but rather one

made of iron, coated with tin. It is the iron, rather than the tin, which is attracted to the magnet.

Those materials which are attracted by the magnet are called magnetic materials; the others are nonmagnetic materials. It is interesting to walk around with a magnet and test various objects which are normally found in a room.

When an object is attracted to the magnet, we can actually feel the pull of magnetism when we try to separate the two. It seems as if some invisible force were trying to hold the two objects together. In the process of separation, it almost feels as if we were stretching a rubber band.

Aside from magnetism, there are other natural forces which can also not be seen, but whose effect is felt every day, for example, the gravitational attraction which the earth exerts on everything on it and which keeps us all from flying off. This is a force we certainly cannot "see." Another is the wind. It can exert a tremendous force, and yet it is completely invisible.

Magnetic Lines

Materials you will need:

1. *At least one magnet (two or three preferred)*
2. *Piece of glass or fairly stiff piece of cardboard*
3. *Iron filings or piece of steel wool*

THE area in space around which a magnet is effective is called its magnetic field. To demonstrate its existence, we brought a magnet close to a magnetic material and saw that even before the magnet touches, an unseen force attracted the material to the magnet. A paper clip and a magnet illustrate this fact simply. We can also very simply make a visible representation of this field.

Lay a magnet under a piece of glass or a stiff piece of carboard. From a height of about 10 inches, sprinkle some iron filings over the area under which the magnet lies. Tap the cardboard gently, and you will see that the filings will take on a distinct pattern (Figure A). This is the pattern of the magnetic

field around the magnet. If the iron filings are dispensed from a salt shaker, they will spread out evenly over the whole area.

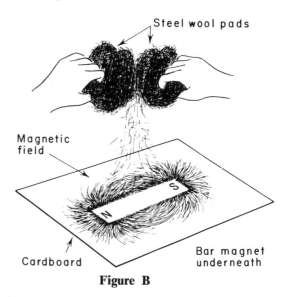

Figure B

The lines which appear are actually the invisible path over which magnetism acts (they were called "magnetic lines" by Michael Faraday). The magnetic field that is filled with these lines extends in all directions around the magnet, not just the one area in which our filings happen to be located. We will show this in the next experiment. All the magnetic lines of force added together are called the *flux* of the magnet.

Iron filings can be readily obtained by using a file on a nail or other iron object and collecting the material that flakes off. If this method is not practical, iron filings can probably be purchased in a local supply house. Another effective way to demonstrate a magnetic field pattern is by using steel wool. It will easily produce the small particles required, and there will be no need for iron filings. Here is how we go about it. Take two small pieces or steel wool, and rub them together with your hands over the cardboard under which the magnetic has been placed (Figure B). Out of these two pieces of steel wool will fall very

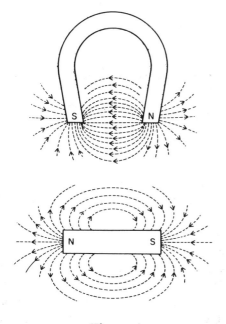

Figure A

small pieces of material, which on their own accord will align themselves along the magnetic lines of force which exist around the magnet. This material is not easily gathered and reused, because it has a tendency to hang together, but two pieces of steel wool will produce a plentiful supply of particles for many experiments.

If you wish to make a permanent record of these field patterns, it can be done in the following way. Place a sheet of wax paper over the cardboard or glass under which the magnet lies, and sprinkle your material on top of the wax paper. When the desired pattern is formed, carefully heat the wax paper so as to melt some of the wax on it. The iron filings will adhere to the softened wax, and if the latter is allowed to harden, you will have a permanent record of the magnetic field.

A heat lamp can be used to heat the paper, but a more even heat can be obtained more quickly by placing the paper into a *warm* oven. Turn off the oven, and let the wax solidify without moving the paper. You will thus avoid taking a chance of disturbing the pattern.

Other interesting magnetic fields can be demonstrated by using combinations of mag-

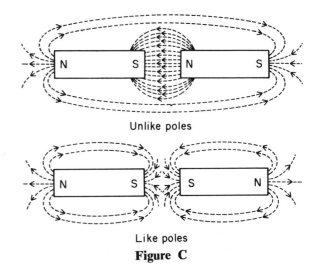

Unlike poles

Like poles

Figure C

nets and thus showing the magnetic field patterns when like poles and unlike poles face each other (Figure C).

When unlike poles are facing each other, the lines of force will extend from the North pole of one of the magnets all the way around to the South pole of the other magnet. On the other hand, when we have like poles facing each other, we will get a different pattern that will extend from the North pole to the South pole of the respective magnets, but where the poles are facing each other, the lines of force will seem to fan out.

Demonstrating Magnetic Lines of Force with a Compass

Materials you will need:

1. *Compass*
2. *Bar magnet*
3. *Piece of paper and a pencil*

WITH a compass and a magnet we can also show those important but really imaginary magnetic lines of force which exist around a magnet. Lay the magnet in the center

of a piece of paper; then place the compass in at least 15 different spots around the magnet about 2 inches away. Note the direction in which the needle is pointing at each spot. For each position draw a small arrow pointing in exactly the same direction as the compass needle does. Keep on moving the compass around the magnet, and you will soon have a drawing very much like the one illustrated in Figure A. If you carefully look at the small

Showing the effect on a compass of a
bar magnet's magnetic field

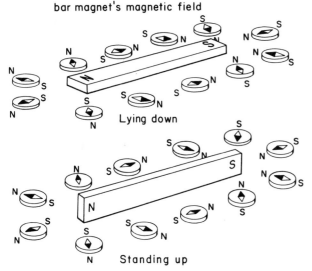

Lying down

Standing up

Figure A

arrows, you will see that they all point away from one pole and towards the other pole, indicating the same direction for all of the magnetic lines of force.

Repeat the same experiment, but this time, move the compass around at a distance of about 3 inches from the magnet. Again you will find that the little arrows point in the same direction as before, showing that here too we have magnetic lines of force. Repeat

the experiment at a farther distance or perhaps try it a little closer to the magnet, and you will see that magnetic lines of force extend in all directions from the magnet.

We can also show that the magnetic lines of force extend not only in this one plane but in all planes. Turn the magnet over on its side or on its edge, and repeat the experiment by again moving the compass all around. You will see that lines of force are again going in the same direction as before. This proves that the magnetic field extends around the magnet in all planes.

If you have two magnets of equal strength, place them about 3 inches apart in the center of a large piece of paper. Move the compass around the two magnets, and draw the arrows. They will show the field pattern that exists around the two magnets.

Stand the bar magnet on one of the poles as illustrated in Figures B and C, and again locate the compass at various spots in a circle around the poles. Interestingly enough, this time the compass will point toward the magnet or away from it regardless of where in the periphery the compass is located. This shows that all around the pole the magnetic lines of force

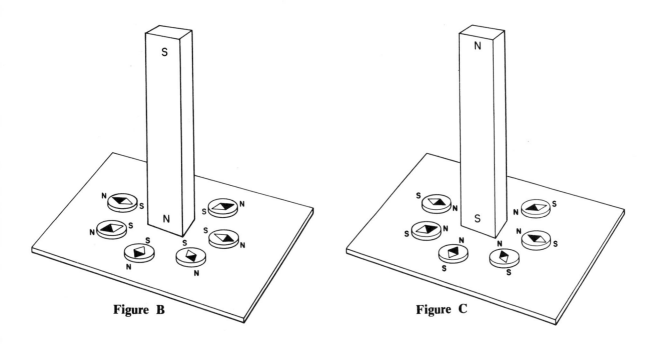

Figure B

Figure C

[45]

go in the same direction. They go *into* the pole if you have a South pole, and *away* from the pole if you have a North pole, resting on the paper. If a bar magnet is not available, this experiment can be perfomed by holding one pole of a horsehoe magnet or other strong magnet onto one end of a long nail or a knitting needle and resting the other end on the paper while moving the magnet all around.

From the above experiments, it is evident that magnetism extends in every possible direction around the poles of a magnet into the surrounding space.

How to Show a Magnetic Field in Three Dimensions

Materials you will need:

1. *Clear plastic or glass container*
2. *Clear salad oil (enough to fill the container)*
3. *Powdered iron or iron filings (a piece of steel wool will also do)*
4. *One or two permanent magnets*

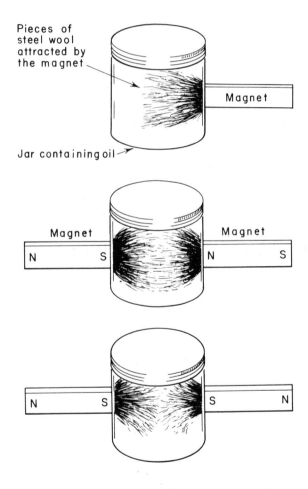

HERE is another interesting way of illustrating a magnetic field. This one will actually reveal the field in three dimensions and provides a much more effective display than the one in the previous experiment.

Rub two pieces of steel wool (the type that does not have soap in it) against each other with your hands. Under the steel wool you should have a piece of paper on which to collect the small pieces of metal which will fall out as a result of the rubbing. Take these little pieces of steel wool (or powdered iron or iron filings, whichever you have), and put them into your container. Then add the oil practically to the top of the container, and put the cover on tightly. Mix the metal with the oil by vigorous shaking.

The material will distribute itself evenly through the oil. Hold one pole of the magnet near the side of the container. The filings will align themselves near the pole and take on the shape of the magnetic field that is present around that pole. Repeat the experiment using the other pole of the magnet, and you will see that the pattern will be the same as before. Now, use two magnets and hold one on each side of the container. The filings will distribute themselves around the two poles of the magnet, and the pattern you obtain will depend on whether you have like or unlike poles facing each other. If you have two unlike poles, the filings will show very clearly the attraction between them, and if you have unlike poles, the tendency to "push apart" will also be shown very clearly. (Keep the container with its oil-particle mixture for future experiments. Remember that it must be shaken before use so as to distribute the particles evenly.)

Making Magnets

Materials you will need:

1. *Alnico (or other strong) magnet*
2. *Sewing needle, steel knitting needle, or large iron nail*
3. *Dozen paper clips*

SOFT iron can be quickly magnetized, but it will lose its magnetism rather easily. Hardened steel or certain steel alloys, on the other hand, though they are magnetized with more difficulty, will retain their magnetism for a much longer time. In a number of experiments which follow, we will need magnetized rods and needles, so be sure to do this experiment, and do it well. We will be talking about sewing needles, but any needle (provided it contains iron) or nail can also be satisfactorily magnetized. If none of these items is available, a straightened paper clip will serve quite well to illustrate the process.

To magnetize the whole needle at once, hold it at one end and rub it with one pole of the magnet about ten times as shown in Figure

A. This is not a back-and-forth but a unidirectional motion. Remove the magnet from the needle each time as soon as you reach the far end.

To magnetize the needle by halves, hold the magnet in one hand and the needle in the other. Stroke the needle *from the middle* to one end with one pole of the permanent magnet. To do this, carefully place the center of the needle against the pole of the magnet, hold the needle there, and pull the magnet out (Figure B). Repeat this about 10 times. Then hold that end of the needle which has now been stroked, and repeat the procedure with the other end of the needle. This time, stroke it an equal number of times with the *other pole* of the magnet. The needle is now magnetized, as you can prove by touching it to a number of paper clips. Of course, they will be attracted to either end of the needle, where we now have produced a North pole and a South pole.

This process of magnetization can be used on any substance which initially is attracted by the magnet. In other words, any material which is magnetic can be magnetized.

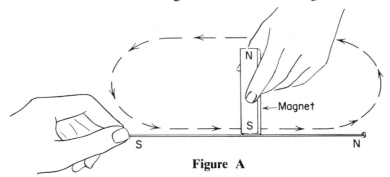

Figure A

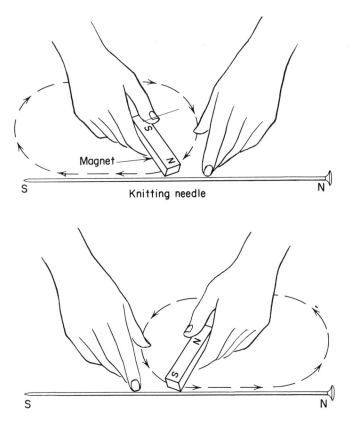

Magnet

Knitting needle

S   N

S   N

Figure B

Though we did not change the outward appearance of the needle, what happened to it to make it behave like a magnet? Materials such as iron and steel are made up of very small particles that act individually like small magnets. Each of them has a North and a South pole, but before the material is magne-

Figure C

tized, these poles all point in different directions. By stroking with the magnet, we essentially line up these elementary magnets and make them all point in the same direction. That is, all the North poles face in one direction, and all the South poles in the other, whereas previously there was no order in their arrangement (Figure C). This alignment of elementary magnets is readily accomplished in some materials and is more difficult in others. In some, this alignment lasts for a long time, and in others it does not. It all depends on the nature of the material we are dealing with.

If you wish to locate the North and South poles in a particular direction, remember that that end of the needle which *last* touched the South pole becomes a North pole, and that end which is rubbed against the North pole becomes a South pole. You can test this polarity with a compass.

Like Poles Repel
and Unlike Poles Attract

Materials you will need:

1. *Magnet*
2. *Sewing needle*
3. *One foot of thread*

MAGNETIZE the sewing needle by stroking it with the magnet, as in the previous experiment. Pass the thread through the eye of the needle, and hang the needle by about 5 inches of thread so that it is free to swing.

Slowly approach the tip of the magnetized needle from underneath with one of the poles of the magnet. One of two things will happen. The needle will either be attracted to the magnet, or it will be repelled. If you approach the tip with a pole of the same polarity, that is to say, if the tip of the needle is a North pole and you approach it with the North pole of the magnet, there will be repulsion, and the needle will tend to fly away. If you then approach the tip with the opposite pole, there will be a strong attraction between the tip and the pole of the magnet. Try not to have the magnet touch the needle during any part of this experiment because as the magnet is removed, there is a possibility that the polarity of the needle's magnetic field will be changed or neutralized, depending on how the magnet is removed from the needle.

This very simple experiment demonstrates one of the basic laws of magnetism, which states that like magnetic poles repel each other and unlike poles attract. We also can clearly see that there is a space all around the magnet where its magnetic force can be felt.

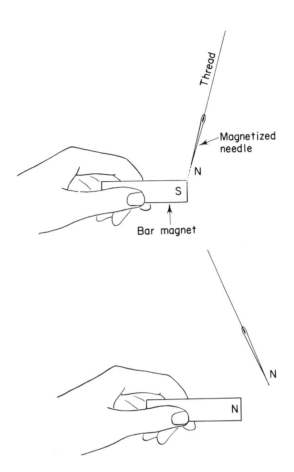

Magnetism Exceeds Gravity 46

Materials you will need:

1. *Magnet*
2. *Paper clip*
3. *Two feet of thin string or thread*

SUSPEND a magnet so that it hangs about one foot above a table. Tie a paper clip to a thin piece of string. Hold the loose end of the string down to the table with a heavy book or other weight, and let the string extend so far that the paper clip will be within a half inch or less of the hanging magnet. Hold the magnet so that it does not swing, and then let go of both the clip and the magnet. Apparently completely contrary to the laws of gravity, the paper clip will remain floating in mid-air without any visible means of support. What actually is happening is that the magnet attracts the clip, but they cannot touch because of the restraining effect of the string.

The stronger the magnet, the greater will be the distance through which it will act on the paper clip. If you make the distance too great, the attractive force of the magnet will not be large enough to overcome the force of gravity, and the clip will fall. If this happens, set the experiment up again. Simply bring the magnet and the clip closer together by lengthening the string you use. You can pass some nonmagnetic materials such as paper, glass, cardboard, or plastic between the floating clip and magnet. These will have no effect. Magnetic lines go right through such materials. Now try some magnetic materials like a thin piece of iron or steel, for example, a knife. The clip will fall, since these materials offer an easy path for magnetism and thus act as a shield. This is yet another way of showing that an invisible force exists around the poles of a magnet that enables it to attract magnetic materials.

You can also demonstrate induced magnetism by hanging another paper clip onto the bottom of the one suspended in mid-air. We see that not only is the first paper clip attracted to the magnet, but it has itself become a magnet as a result of induced magnetism and therefore exerts an attractive force on the second paper clip. Try now to add a third clip.

This last experiment clearly shows that a piece of iron or steel can become magnetized by induction not only when it is in contact with a magnet, but also when it is only brought close to it.

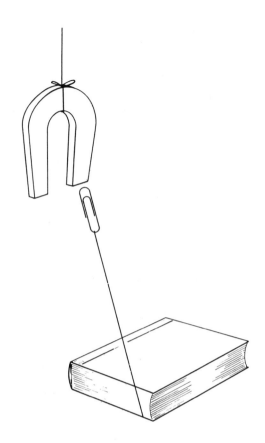

Which Magnet is Stronger?

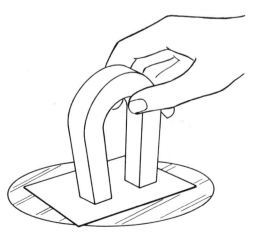

Materials you will need:

1. *Tin can cover*
2. *Magnets*
3. *Twenty small pieces of paper*

THE cover from a tin can can help us measure the comparative strength of magnets. Prepare about 15 or 20 pieces of paper slightly larger than the poles of the magnet. First using one piece, and then increasing one at a time, see how many pieces of paper you can put between each magnet and the cover (thus increasing the distance between the two) and still have the magnet attract the cover. That magnet which can still lift the cover through the greatest number of paper squares (that is, through the greatest distance) is the stronger.

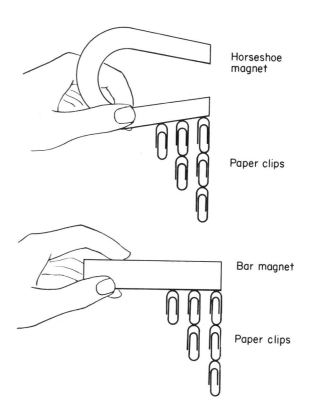

Pieces of paper

Tin can cover

Where is a Magnet the Strongest?

Materials you will need:

1. *Number of paper clips*
2. *Number of small nails*
3. *Magnet*

TO find out where a magnet has its greatest strength, bring it close to a number of paper clips or small nails which lie in a pile. You will see that some of them will be attracted by the magnet. Try various other spots on the magnet, and see where the magnet picks up the most pieces. You will soon find that the ends of the magnet which are called the poles pick up the greatest number of paper clips or nails. Therefore, the poles are where a magnet is the strongest.

Another way to demonstrate where a magnet has its greatest strength is illustrated. Here we support a chain of several small paper clips. As we go farther away from the poles (even a short distance), fewer and fewer pieces will be held up until we reach a point between the poles at which there will be no attraction whatsoever. Here again we show

Horseshoe magnet

Paper clips

Bar magnet

Paper clips

that the strongest attraction is near the ends or poles of the magnet.

Induced and Residual Magnetism

Materials you will need:
1. *Number of paper clips*
2. *Magnet*

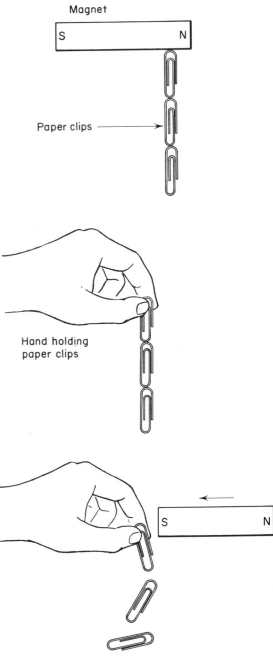

Magnet

Paper clips

Hand holding
paper clips

WHEN a magnet is brought near a magnetic material, its influence is such that the point of the material closest to the magnet will take on a polarity opposite that of the end of the magnet facing it. Since opposite poles attract each other, the magnet and the material will be attracted to each other even though the material itself is not a magnet. As we found out in Experiment 44, every molecule of the material will align itself in the direction of the magnetic field. As soon as the magnet is removed, the molecules will again orient themselves in the helter-skelter manner in which they were previously. The magnetism which existed in the material was thus only temporary. That is, it was induced at the time the material was in contact with the magnet. We can prove this very simply.

Hold a paper clip against one of the poles of a magnet. If you touch the other end of this clip with another clip, that second clip, as we saw in the previous experiment, will be held

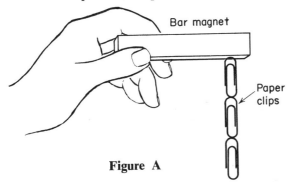

Bar magnet

Paper clips

Figure A

fast to the first by magnetic attraction (Figure A). Perhaps a third clip can be hung on to the second, and so on. This happens because our magnet *induces* magnetism in the clip which is held to it. This clip in turn induces magnetism in the second clip, so that it too becomes

Figure B

a magnet and thus is able to attract the third clip. As soon as you remove the magnet, the clips will probably separate. We say probably, because whether they separate or not depends on the *retentivity* of the material of which the clip is made.

Retentivity is a term which indicates how long a substance will retain its magnetism after the magnetizing force is removed. If two clips still stick together, this indicates that the magnetism in at least one of them did not completely disappear and that the molecules maintained their alignment after the inducing magnet was removed. The magnetism which remains as the result of the retentivity of the material is called *residual magnetism.*

If you now slowly approach that end of the clip from which the magnet was removed with *the other pole* of the magnet (Figure B), you will see that even before it touches the clips, they will separate. This happens because you are now inducing magnetism of the oppo-site polarity, and the other end of the clip will now have a polarity which is the same as that of the clip which it is holding up. We know that like poles repel, so the clips will separate.

Another way of showing induced magnet-ism is to dip one end of a soft iron bar or nail into some iron filings (Figure C). The filings will not stick to the nail when you pull it out. Bring a permanent magnet near the top of the iron nail while it is submerged in the iron fil-ings (you don't have to touch the nail with

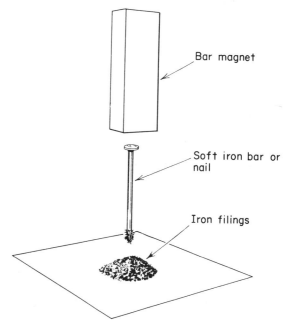

Bar magnet

Soft iron bar or nail

Iron filings

Figure C

the magnet; just bring it near as shown). Then lift the magnet and the nail, and you will see that some of the filings will stick to the nail. Move the magnet away, and the iron will lose most of its magnetism. Most of the filings will drop off. Those that stick will do so because of the residual magnetism of the nail. Turn the magnet over, approach the nail again, and the filings will fall off for reasons explained ear-lier in this experiment.

Proving the Theory of Magnetism 50

> **Materials you will need:**
>
> 1. *Test tube, long narrow jar, or tooth brush tube*
> 2. *Permanent magnet*
> 3. *Compass (a ten cent compass from a variety store will do)*
> 4. *Iron filings or piece of steel wool*

WE stated earlier that when a material be-comes magnetized, all of its molecules align themselves in the same direction. We can prove this theory with an experiment.

Fill a small test tube or narrow jar about half way with iron filings or steel wool pieces produced in the same way as in earlier ex-periments. These little pieces of material are analogous to molecules. Bring the bottom of the test tube near a compass. It will attract either end of the needle as would any other magnetic substance. Now stroke the test tube from one end to the other with the pole of a strong magnet (Figure A) and then bring the test tube again near the compass (Figure B).

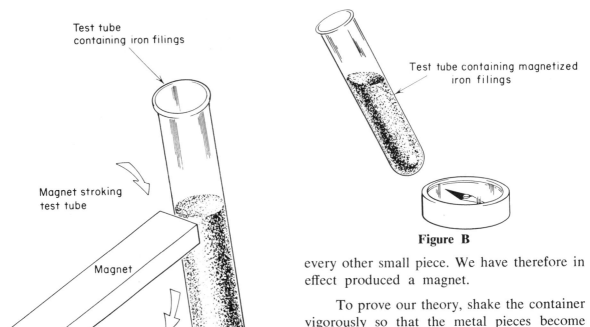

Test tube
containing iron filings

Magnet stroking
test tube

Magnet

Figure A

Test tube containing magnetized
iron filings

Figure B

You will find that it will now act like a magnet and thus attract one end of the needle but repel the other. What happened is that each small piece has been lined up with its North pole pointing in the same direction as that of

every other small piece. We have therefore in effect produced a magnet.

To prove our theory, shake the container vigorously so that the metal pieces become disarranged and again bring it near the compass. This time it will behave as it had before we magnetized it. Shaking the metal pieces breaks up their uniform magnetic alignment.

It is experiments such as this one that first led scientists to believe that magnetism results from the alignment of small pieces of a material such as its molecules.

51   Heat Destroys Magnetism

Materials you will need:

1. *Compass*
2. *Sewing needle*
3. *Source of heat (matches)*
4. *Pair of pliers*

PLACE the compass on a drinking glass or any other nonmagnetic material which keeps it about 4 inches or more above the surface on which you are working. Hold the needle in a pair of pliers. Bring the free end close to

one end of the compass needle. Then bring it close to the other. The needle will attract both poles equally.

Now magnetize the needle by stroking it with a magnet as we have done in an earlier experiment. Again hold the magnetized needle in the pliers, and approach the compass from a direction which is at right angles to the one in which the compass is pointing. That is, since the compass is pointing North, approach it either from the East or West. This time only one pole will be attracted to the needle. The other will be repelled because the needle is now a magnet.

Now bring a match or other flame under the needle, and hold it there for a few seconds. Hold the needle once more near the compass, and you will see that it will again attract both poles as it did before we magnetized it. The needle is not a magnet anymore.

What we have done here is to prove one of the theories of magnetism. It states that heat will cause the molecules in a magnetized material to become rearranged in a helter-skelter manner and that the material will thus lose its magnetism since the molecular poles are no longer pointing in the same direction.

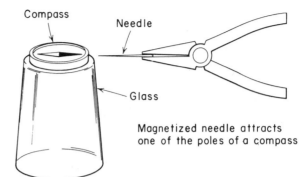

Magnetized needle attracts one of the poles of a compass

Making a Floating Compass

Materials you will need:

1. *Large sewing needle*
2. *Cork*
3. *Permanent magnet*
4. *Glass, cup, or other nonmagnetic container of water*
5. *Detergent*

THE first practical use for magnetism was in a compass. In a few minutes we can make a compass which will be as good as any of those by which men steered their ships for centuries. Before the word compass came into use, these instruments were given such curious names as "floating iron fish." Their heads always pointed North, and their tails pointed South. It took our ancestors many centuries to discover the North-South pointing property of a magnet and make practical use of it.

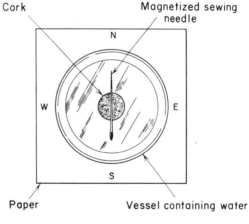

Figure A

The earliest mariner's compasses were known as "gnomons" and consisted of a magnetized steel needle which was pushed through a short piece of wood and floated on the surface of a vessel containing water. This floating arrangement was set spinning, and as soon as it came to rest, the needle aligned itself in the

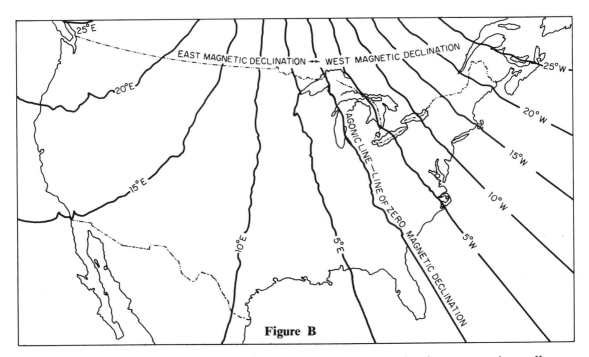

EAST MAGNETIC DECLINATION ← → WEST MAGNETIC DECLINATION

AGONIC LINE—LINE OF ZERO MAGNETIC DECLINATION

25° E, 20° E, 15° E, 10° E, 5° E, 25° W, 20° W, 15° W, 10° W, 5° W

Figure B

North and South direction. The skipper then proceeded accordingly. Our present day compass, though somewhat refined mechanically, still operates essentially on this principle.

We know now that a compass needle is actually a magnet, supported so that it is free to turn. We can provide this freedom in a number of ways. One of the simplest is to magnetize a sewing needle and with the help of a cork float it in water. Here is how:

Magnetize a sewing needle as we have done in a previous experiment by stroking it with a magnet. Cut a flat section from a cork about ¼ inch thick, and lay the magnetized needle upon the cork so that the needle will float horizontally (Figure A). Float the cork with the needle in a water-filled glass, a china bowl,

a cup, or an aluminum pan. A small amount of detergent should be mixed with the water to lower the surface tension of the water. This keeps the cork and the needle from moving over towards the edge of the vessel. Give the floating cork a gentle spin, and you will note that it will soon come to rest with the needle pointing in a North and South direction. Turn it in another direction, and it will again return to the same position as before.

A few words of caution are in order at this point. In order for this experiment to be a success, you must be sure that no magnet is lying near the floating compass so as to interfere with its operation. Also, the container you use must not be made of iron or some other magnetic material. Either of these conditions will prevent the compass from functioning. If you bring the magnet you used to magnetize the sewing needle close to the little float, it will attract one pole if opposite poles are facing but will repel if you have a North pole facing a North pole or a South pole facing a South pole.

The cork you use should be no thicker than ¼ inch. The cork lining from the cap of a soda pop bottle is quite suitable for our pur-

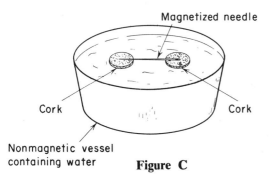

Magnetized needle

Cork   Cork

Nonmagnetic vessel
containing water   **Figure C**

pose. If you use this, then first float the little piece of cork on the water and then carefully place the needle on top of it.

This compass can actually be put to use. Take a piece of paper several inches larger than the container for the water, and mark "North" on the top of it, "South" on the bottom of it, "East" on the right side, and "West" on the left side. Then set the container of water with the floating cork on top of the paper, and let the needle come to rest. When the needle stops turning, lift the vessel carefully, and move the paper until the North pointer on the paper corresponds to the northerly direction in which the compass is pointing. This will then be the magnetic North pole.

The actual location of the geographic North pole does not coincide with the magnetic North pole, and some correction must be made. Around the New York area the geographic North pole is about 10° west of the magnetic North towards which our compass is pointing (an angle known as the angle of magnetic declination), and in the Los Angeles area the geographic North pole is about 18° east of the magnetic North (Figure B shows the distribution of declination in the United States).

There is another way of making a floating compass. For this we require two thin slices of cork and a magnetized needle. Stick the point of the needle into one of the corks and the eye into the other, as illustrated in Figure C. This compass is somewhat easier to construct and will stand rougher treatment than the needle floating on a single cork. It is said that this type of compass was used around the time Columbus discovered America.

A Different Kind of Compass

Materials you will need:

1. *Piece of paper about 2 x 5 inches*
2. *Sewing needle*
3. *Two paper clips (or two needles)*
4. *Cork*
5. *Permanent magnet*

FOLD the paper in half lengthwise so that it makes a little roof as shown in Figure A. Straighten out the paper clips and push them (or two needles) through the paper on each side. Now lay the paper flat on the table, and magnetize the two paper clips by stroking them with the magnet about 20 times, beginning at one end and ending at the other. (After stroking in one direction, lift the magnet each time and go back and stroke again in the same direction with the same pole of the magnet.) Each clip will now have a North pole

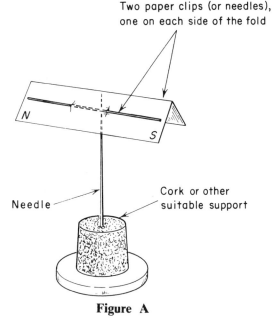

Figure A

and a South pole, with the North pole of each at the same end, provided you have stroked them both in the same direction and with the same pole of the magnet.

Put a sewing needle through the center of the cork with the point up, and balance the folded piece of paper on the needle point, being very careful not to pierce the paper. Balance it in the center, so that it will swing freely. Be sure to keep the magnet you used far out of the way, and give the paper a little twist so that it will spin around once or twice. It will then come to rest pointing in one direction. Twist it again and you will see that it will come to rest in the same direction. One end will point North and the other will point South. Mark the letter "N" on the side that points towards the North and the letter "S" on the side that points to the South. We have now made a compass, which can be readily taken apart and stored for use any time a compass is required. Simple as it is, it is a very accurate and sensitive instrument and perhaps has greater precision than the compasses which our forefathers used for many, many centuries.

You can magnetize another paper clip, and illustrate the laws of magnetic attraction and repulsion with this compass. It is not advisable to bring a strong permanent magnet such as the one which we used to magnetize the paper clips originally close to this compass, because of the fact that a strong magnet will have such great effect that it might pull the paper right off its support or even magnetize the clips in an opposite direction. If you want to experiment with a permanent magnet and this compass, be sure to keep the magnet at a respectable distance.

If you wish to use this compass outdoors, it must be protected from the wind. There are

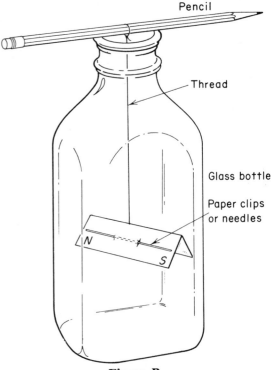

Figure B

two ways of doing so. One is to cover the whole assembly with a wide-mouthed jar so it will be protected all around. Another, and perhaps preferable way, is to support the folded paper from a very fine thread through a hole in the center where the point of the upright needle had been formerly. The thread should be passed through the paper and a knot made on the underside. The other end of the string should be tied around a pencil or a toothpick. The whole assembly can then be dropped into a bottle or a jar so that the paper with the magnetized clips hangs inside, held in place and supported by the pencil across the opening of the bottle (Figure B). Test this compass to be sure that it swings freely and aligns in a North-South direction.

Magnetic Poles Can Be Anywhere

Materials you will need:
1. Compass
2. Paper clip
3. Magnet

THE poles of a magnet need not always be located at its end; neither do the ends of a magnet have to be opposite poles. We can have a magnet with poles at each end that are of the same polarity. That is, we can have two

South poles or two North poles. Of course, these are not isolated South poles or North poles without their equal and opposite poles. The arrangement is somewhat like that illustrated. We have now what are called *consecutive poles*. In other words, instead of having a sequence going South-North-South-North, we can have South-North-North-South. We can produce this arrangement very simply.

Straighten a paper clip, bring it near the compass, and check it all along its length to see that it is unmagnetized. This can be proved by showing that either of the poles of the magnet can be attracted to the paper clip at any point. When it is clear the clip is not magnetized, touch one of the poles of your magnet to the center of the clip, and remove the magnet without sliding it towards either end of the clip. Now check the clip again for polarity (using any of the compasses you now have) and you will find out to your surprise that *both ends* of the clip are of the *same polarity*. If you touched the center of the clip with the South pole, both ends will be South poles. The North

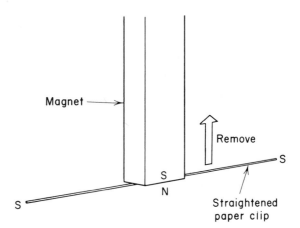

poles of course will be located next to each other in the center of the clip, where the South pole of the magnet was previously attached. If the North pole of the magnet is used, all of the polarities of course become reversed.

Fold this magnetized paper clip in half, and you will have in essence a horseshoe magnet whose two ends are of the same polarity. Assuming that you have two South poles, the North poles will be located in the center at the bend of the magnet.

The Earth as a Magnet

55

THE fact that a compass needle aligns itself in a particular direction at every point on the earth tells us that the earth is surrounded by a magnetic field, almost as if there were a huge bar magnet running through its center. One pole, called the North magnetic pole, is up near the North geographic pole (actually about 1,400 miles away), and the other pole, called the South magnetic pole, is near the geographic South pole (also about 1,400 miles away). The precise distance of the magnetic poles from the geographic poles changes somewhat from time to time.

We know now that if the North pole of a magnet is free to turn, it will come to rest pointing towards what has been designated as the North magnetic pole. But we also know that unlike poles attract. Therefore we see that

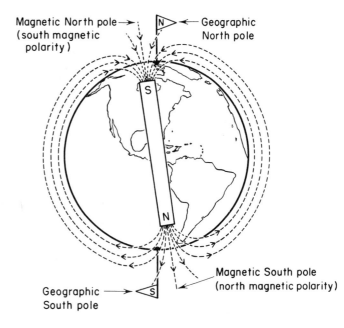

the North magnetic pole of the earth is actually a magnetic South pole. (Likewise, the earth's South magnetic pole is in actuality a magnetic North pole.)

Queen Elizabeth's physician, William Gilbert, did indeed claim around the year 1600 that the earth was a magnet. He proved it by shaping a lodestone in the form of the earth and showed that a compass, when moved around this lodestone, behaved essentially the same way as does a compass when moved on the earth.

Magnetic Dip or Inclination

56

Materials you will need:

1. *Bar magnet*
2. *Piece of paper*
3. *Knitting needle*
4. *Cork*
5. *Two glasses*
6. *Darning needle*

THE magnetic field of the earth is not only felt in a North-South direction but also at an angle towards the earth. The strength of the earth's magnetism varies from a maximum at the poles to a minimum at the equator. The strength at any point is measured with a dip needle. This is essentially a compass type of indicator that is pivoted so it can be moved vertically rather than horizontally as the compass does.

First of all, let us demonstrate why we get a magnetic dip and what it really is. Take a bar magnet, or a magnetized needle, and place it in the center of a piece of paper. Draw a circle around this magnet about 4 inches larger in diameter than the length of the magnet. Draw a line through the center of the circle so that it also goes through the center of the magnet. Mark the top of the circle "N" and the bottom "S." Then draw 12 circles (somewhat larger than the compass which you are using) all around the "earth" as shown in Figure A. With the magnet in place, locate the compass in each of these positions, and note

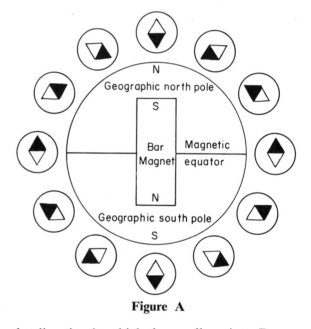

Figure A

the direction in which the needle points. Draw a little pointer in the direction of the needle after removing the compass. It takes very little imagination to realize that if we were to mount a magnetized needle so that it can swivel in a vertical plane, it would point straight down at the North and South poles and be parallel to the ground along the magnetic equator. At all other points, it would have a certain amount of inclination. We can illustrate this very simply.

Push a steel knitting needle lengthwise through a cork, and stick a darning needle through the cork in an opposite direction. It is most important that the knitting needle *not* be magnetized at this time. Adjust the knitting needle so that it will balance perfectly in a horizontal direction when allowed to swivel on the darning needle, which is supported on the rim of two glasses. This is a delicate but important adjustment (Figure B).

Now, without changing the position of either needle in the cork, magnetize the knitting needle by stroking it with a magnet from the cork out, first in one direction, and then in the other. The second time, of course, the opposite pole of the magnet should be used. We are thus magnetizing the needle strongly, giving it a North pole at one end and a South pole at the other.

Carefully replace the assembly on the rim of the glasses, and watch what happens. This time, one side of the knitting needle will definitely point downward at an angle from the horizontal (unless, of course, you happen to be located at the magnetic equator). In the northern hemisphere it will be the north-seeking pole. The closer you come to either pole,

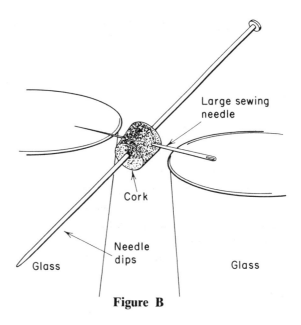

Figure B

the steeper will be the inclination, and the nearer the equator, the more parallel the needle will be to the ground. (Figure C shows the angle of inclination for all latitudes of the world.)

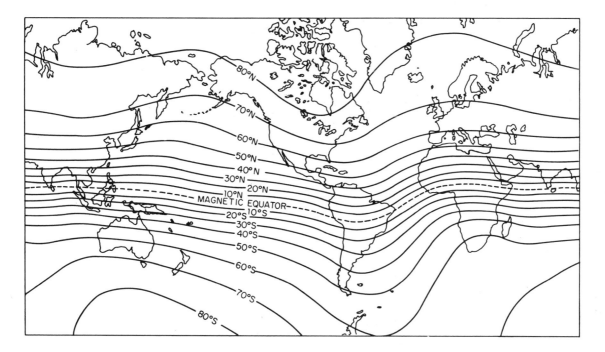

Figure C

Magnetism from the Earth's Field

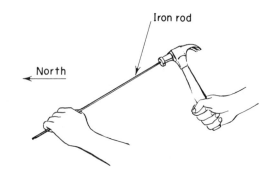

Materials you will need:

1. *Iron rod or large bolt*
2. *Hammer*
3. *Compass*

WE know that the earth acts as a huge magnet. As a result, pieces of iron or steel which lie in a North-South direction often become magnetized by induction. If such objects are jolted while in this position, their molecules line up and they become more easily magnetized. We can thus magnetize some materials by tapping them with a hammer.

Gently tap one end of an iron rod or bolt about 20 times while holding it in a North-South position. Best results are obtained if we make sure that the rod is located along the earth's magnetic lines of force. Therefore, as we learned from the previous experiment, tilt the north end of the rod downward if you are in the Northern Hemisphere and the south end downward if you are in the Southern Hemis-

phere before you tap it. You may find that you will have to try various angles of inclination before you have properly aligned the rod with the earth's magnetic line of force.

To prove that the rod is magnetized, see if it will pick up some pins or bring its ends near a compass. If the rod is magnetized, the same point of the compass will be attracted by one end of the rod and repelled by the other. To reverse the poles, turn the rod over and tap the other end. The rod can also be demagnetized by tapping it while it is held in an East-West direction.

Proving a Theory

Materials you will need:

1. *Compass*
2. *Paper clip*
3. *Magnet*
4. *Wire cutter or clippers*

IF the earth's magnetism is so strong, why can't we use it to do some work? We know that the North pole attracts a North-seeking pole, so why not make a very strong North-seeking pole, attach it to some vehicle, and let the earth's magnetism pull it to the North pole?

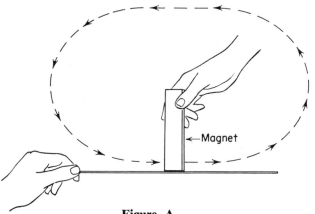

Figure A

That sounds good, so let us try to make an independent North-seeking pole.

First magnetize a piece of steel wire, such as a straight paper clip. Stroke over its entire length with a magnet as illustrated in Figure A for about 20 to 30 strokes. Then test the polarity of this wire with the compass, and you will see that you have produced a North pole and a South pole. So far, so good.

Now let's cut this wire in half. It would seem we would end up with a North pole on one half of the wire, and a South pole on the other half of the wire. But alas, upon testing the two halves of the wire with a compass, we find that each of them has a North and a South pole. So let's cut the wire again. Of

course, the magnet this time will be a smaller one, but it still has a North pole on one end and a South pole on the other.

Thus we have found out one of the basic laws of magnetism, which states that *every magnet has (at least) two poles*. It is impossible to produce a magnet with only one pole. No matter how small we make it, we will always have a North pole and a South pole. Therefore, we cannot create an independent North-seeking pole, and the vehicle we mentioned above is thus impossible.

This phenomenon can also be very simply demonstrated by breaking a horseshoe magnet of the dime store variety into a number of pieces (Figure B).

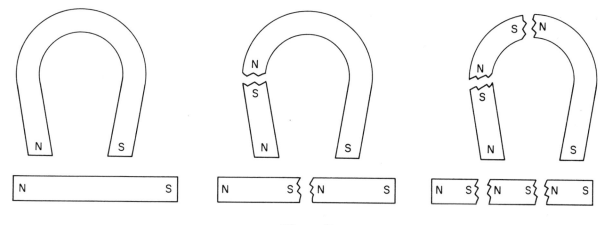

Figure B

Which One is Magnetized? 59

Materials you will need:

1. *Two identical rods or knitting needles (in a pinch, two large sewing needles or nails will do)*
2. *Magnet*

HERE is an old-time favorite problem in magnetism. With the knowledge we have gained so far, it should be very simple to solve,

but it may prove to be quite a challenge to the uninformed.

Magnetize one, and only one, of the knitting needles by rubbing it across its length with a magnet, as we have done in earlier experiments. Be sure that the two needles you have are exactly alike, except of course that one of them is now magnetized. Ask anyone to tell you with certainty which one of the two is the magnetized one. Both will attract each other at their ends, no matter which you use to touch the other. When everyone gives up, here is how you distinguish between them.

Touch the tip of one of the two to the center of the other. If there is attraction, then the one whose tip you used is the magnetized one, and the other is unmagnetized. If there is no attraction, use the tip of the other one to touch the center of the first, note that there is now attraction, and identify the second one as being the magnetized one. Here is what is happening:

We know that the strength of a magnet is concentrated near its ends (the poles) with no magnetic strength at the center. Therefore, since no magnetism exists in the center, there

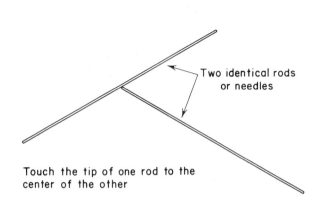

Two identical rods or needles

Touch the tip of one rod to the center of the other

will be attraction only if we touch the center with a magnetized material.

60 Rescuing the Paper Clip

Materials you will need:

1. *Glass of water*
2. *Paper clip*
3. *Magnet*

FILL a glass with water and drop a paper clip into it. Now challenge anyone to remove the paper clip without spilling the water or inserting anything into it. Actually it is a very simple trick.

When everyone gives up, you hold the glass in one hand and a magnet in the other. Bring the magnet to the undersurface of the glass, near the paper clip. We know that magnetism will act through glass, so the paper clip will be attracted by the magnet. Once you have accomplished this, the rest is very simple. Guide the paper clip up the side of the glass by sliding the magnet along the outer surface

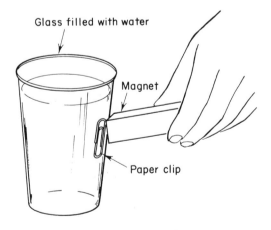

Glass filled with water

Magnet

Paper clip

of the glass so that the paper clip remains attracted to it. Once you have reached the surface, the paper clip will jump onto the magnet when you bring it beyond the lip of the glass.

Magnetic Separation

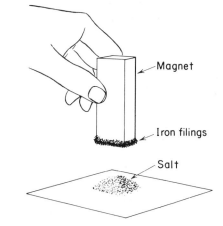

HERE is an interesting little stunt which will serve to illustrate magnetism. Mix together some iron filings and a little bit of salt. Then ask anyone to separate the two materials quickly and easily. Of course, you can use water to dissolve the salt and evaporate the water to recover the salt, but there is a much easier way. It is not as difficult as it may sound.

Stir the mixture with the permanent magnet. You will find that the iron filings will be attracted to the magnet, but the salt will not.

Thus we can readily pull the iron filings away from the salt. This is essentially the process used in industry to separate magnetic substances from those which are nonmagnetic.

How to Tell Time with a Compass

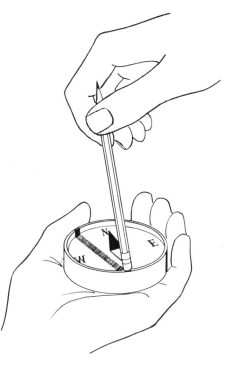

THIS is a simple way of telling the approximate time on a sunny day. Here is how you do it. Determine which direction is North by using your compass. Then face in a northerly direction. Holding the compass in one hand, rest the pencil or stick directly above the "S" on its face, tilting it at an angle of about 45°. Let us now assume that the "N" on the compass is 12 o'clock, making the "E" 3 o'clock, the "W" 9 o'clock, and the "S" 6 o'clock. That point at which the shadow falls on the compass will give you the approximate standard time of the day. This way of telling time is similar to the way a sun dial operates. Of course, in order for this experiment to be successful, we must have sunlight.

Making Floating Magnets

Materials you will need:

1. *Four sewing needles*
2. *Cork*
3. *Magnet*
4. *Nonmagnetic container of water such as an aluminum pie dish or a large plastic dish*

MAGNETIZE the sewing needles as we have done many times, being sure that their magnetic fields are all in the same direction. That is to say, all the points of the needles should be of one polarity and all the eyes of the other.

Cut four thin slices from the cork, each about ¼ inch thick. Push a needle halfway through each slice of cork, and float the slices so that the eyes of the needles will be in and the points out of the water. Each of the needles is now a floating magnet, with one of its poles in the water and the other outside of the water.

Arrange the little floats so that they are essentially in a square. If you try to push them close together, they will not stay that way but will repel each other since we know that like magnetic poles repel. (A small amount of detergent can be mixed into the water to reduce surface tension.)

Now hold one of the poles of the magnet above the center of the floating magnets. One of two things will happen. If the points of the needle sticking out of the water are North poles, and if you approach with the North pole of the magnet, the floats will be further separated. If you approach with the South pole, they will be attracted toward the center. The same, of course, holds true if all the points sticking out are South poles. That is, if you approach with a South pole, the floats will go further apart, and if you approach with a North pole, they will be attracted toward the center.

If you carefully maneuver the magnet so that the needles are attracted, they will come together up to the point where their mutual repulsion is counterbalanced and offset by the attraction of the magnet.

If the magnet is very strong, the floats will be brought together very closely. With a little bit of care you should be able to form a nice square with these floating magnets. If you take one out and arrange the rest so that there are three corners, you should be able to form a triangle.

The same reaction to the presence of the magnet can also be demonstrated if you approach from underneath the water container rather than from above. This will make for a somewhat more interesting and mystifying experiment if you can show that for no visible reason the boats suddenly converge upon the center and then separate (as the magnet is re-

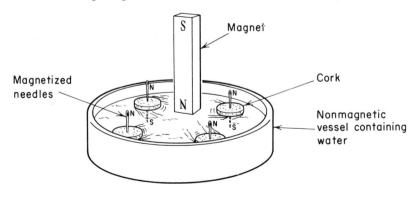

Magnet

Magnetized needles

Cork

Nonmagnetic vessel containing water

moved) and then reconverge (as the magnet is again brought close to the bottom).

If you now turn one or two of the corks upside down so that the eye of the needle is now outside the water instead of the point, you will see that the floats which were not turned around will now be attracted. This of course is due to the fact that unlike magnetic poles attract each other.

How Steady Are You?

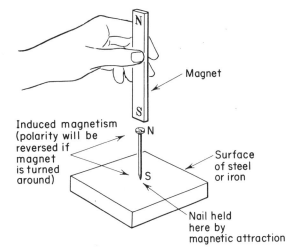

Materials you will need:

1. *Magnet*
2. *Sewing needle or nail*
3. *Steel or iron surface*

TO test your nerves here is a little stunt, which might even be used at a party. See how long you can balance a needle or nail in an upright position using only a magnet to hold it up.

Stand a needle vertically on a piece of steel or iron, and hold your magnet slightly above it. With a little patience you can soon learn to let go of the needle just at the point where the magnetism from the magnet, held in the other hand, will be sufficient to keep the needle standing. This may take a little practice, but it can be done. Be sure not to let the magnet touch the needle or come too close, because then the needle will jump up to it, and that is not what we are trying to accomplish.

You must use a magnetic surface of steel or iron so that the end of the needle which rests on that surface will be held to it by in-

duced magnetism. Otherwise (and you should try it), the needle will jump up to the magnet.

Once you have the needle standing, you can move the magnet back and forth with a slight swaying motion, and you will see that the needle will follow.

To test the steadiness of your hand and nerves, see how long you can keep the needle upright or how far you can make it tilt. If you find this trick too hard using a needle, then try a nail on its point.

Building a Simple Motor

Materials you will need:

1. *Magnet*
2. *Compass*
3. *Two-foot piece of string*

THIS experiment describes about the simplest type of motor we can build. It also illustrates the principle which is used in many larger motors. Suspend a magnet with a piece of string so that it is free to spin as shown in

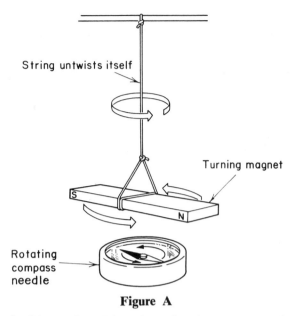

String untwists itself

Turning magnet

S   N

Rotating
compass
needle

Figure A

The compass needle will turn as long as the magnet revolves. When the magnet stops, and the string then twists itself in the opposite direction, the compass needle will follow and also turn in the opposite direction.

The principle we just illustrated is used in a practical way to mix liquids. A magnet is rotated by a motor underneath a nonmagnetic (usually glass) container which holds the liquid to be mixed. Also in this container and resting on the bottom is a small bar magnet. As the motor turns the first magnet, the bar magnet in the liquid will also spin and thereby agitate the solution (Figure B).

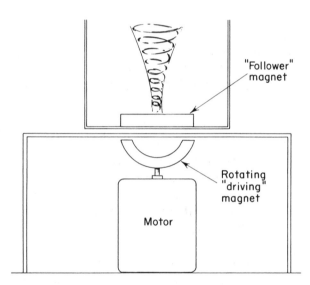

"Follower"
magnet

Rotating
"driving"
magnet

Motor

Figure B

the illustration. Directly under the magnet and a few inches away from it, place the compass so that its needle is also free to spin. The exact distance between the magnet and the compass depends on the strength of the magnet. The stronger the magnet, the greater can be the separation.

To get our little motor going, give the string with the magnet attached about 20 to 30 twists and let it go. As the string untwists and turns the magnet, the compass needle will follow it and also turn (Figure A). This rotation is brought about by the attraction of the poles of the magnet and the respective opposite poles of the compass needle.

66

Build an Eddy Current Motor

Materials you will need:

1. Strong magnet
2. Small aluminum pie plate
3. Sewing needle
4. Cork
*5. Two feet of thin string or heavy
     thread*

WE found out earlier that a piece of aluminum or copper will not be attracted by a magnet. Nevertheless, we will be able to show in this experiment that a magnet can indeed exert a force of some sort on these metals.

Push a sewing needle through a cork so that its point sticks up. Balance an aluminum foil pan of the type used for a small frozen cake or pie on the needle point so that it is level and free to spin (an aluminum or copper disk can also be used if more readily available). Tie a strong horseshoe magnet to a piece of string about 2 feet long. The exact length of the string is not too important. Hold the string so that the magnet is free to spin very closely over the center of the aluminum pan. Note the illustration. Now twist the string about 30 times, carefully holding the magnet so that it remains steady over the center of the pan, and then let the string go. As the magnet spins, it will induce electric currents called *eddy currents* in the aluminum. The eddy currents in turn will produce a magnetic field on top of the aluminum. This field, affected by the field of the magnet, will make the pan turn in the direction in which the magnet is spinning. The faster the magnet spins, the greater will be the magnetic field which is built up in the pan, and the faster the pan will spin. (We will explain in the third section of this book how currents produce a magnetic field.)

The speedometer of an automobile operates on this principle. As the car moves, a magnet is rotated at a speed depending on the speed of the car. The magnet in turn exerts a drag on a piece of metal attached to a pointer on a scale. This pointer indicates the speed at which the car is moving. A hair spring restricts the pointer movement and thus keeps it

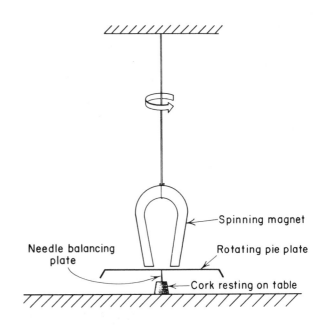

from revolving as our little motor does. But as we just found out, the faster the magnet spins, the greater will be the drag. Therefore the faster our car moves, the farther over the speedometer pointer will swing.

Can Magnetism Be Shielded by Nonmagnetic Materials?

Materials you will need:

1. Magnet
2. Several paper clips

WE know that a magnet will attract paper clips directly, but will it also attract them if there are any intervening materials? Let us find out. Put the paper clips on a piece of cardboard, and the magnet underneath. See if you can attract the paper clips and move them around by moving the magnet. You will see that you can.

Take a piece of wood, put a paper clip on top of it, the magnet underneath, and try the same thing. Try the experiment with some plastic, a glass, a piece of material, a book (if the magnet is not strong enough to exert a force through the whole book, open it half way), a deep plate filled with water, and any other materials you might think of. You will see that a magnet can act through glass, fabric, plastic, paper, water, leather, rubber, cork, in fact through anything which in itself is not acted upon by magnetism, that is, through any nonmagnetic material.

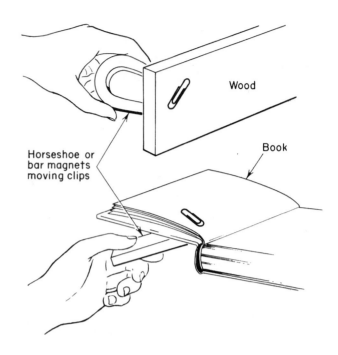

Horseshoe or bar magnets moving clips

Wood

Book

Magnetic Shielding

Materials you will need:

1. *Two magnets*
2. *Compass*
3. *Some high permeability material which will fit around the compass (see text)*

IT has long been determined, and we showed in the previous experiment, that magnetic lines of force will penetrate any nonmagnetic material. Nonmagnetic materials such as glass, copper, or wool allow magnetic lines of force to pass through them very freely, whereas magnetic substances, such as iron and steel, are frequently used as barriers to prevent the penetration of magnetic lines of force. It is oftentimes necessary or desirable to shield certain sensitive instruments and keep magnetic lines away from them. When this is necessary, we can make use of the fact that some magnetic materials concentrate magnetic lines of force.

In order to shield something, we put a good conductor of magnetism all around it so that the lines of force will take the *easy path* through the shield rather than the more difficult one through the air, which would allow them to go through the material we wish to shield. The lines of force will always follow the easiest magnetic path.

To illustrate this phenomenon, place a compass inside a "tin" can. The compass should rest about the center of the can on a little support which can be made out of any nonmagnetic material. Now place the two magnets on opposite sides of the can with unlike poles facing so that under normal circumstances there would be magnetic lines of force going straight through the can and thus influencing the compass. You'll perhaps notice a slight effect on the compass when the magnets are brought into position. This is due to the fact that the permeability of an ordinary tin can isn't quite good enough for this experiment.

To make the experiment more successful, place this tin can into another of larger diameter and check again. If the shielding is still not as effective as you would like it to be, place the two cans into a still larger one. You will find that the magnetic effect will be progressively lessened as we interpose more and more high permeability shields.

Here is another way of showing the effect of a high permeability material. Place the compass about 10 inches away from the magnet, and note the effect the magnet has on the compass needle. Then put some materials between the magnet and the compass, and test the shielding effect. If you try paper, wool,

copper, wood, glass, or any other nonmagnetic material, you will see that there will be no noticeable effect. Now try a magnetic material such as the tin can we used previously. If you allow the magnet to touch the can, you will see that it will effectively "short-circuit" the magnetic field, because of the easier magnetic path it offers, and thus prevent the lines of force from going through and reaching out to the compass.

Sensitive electrical coils in measuring instruments or in radio circuits are oftentimes placed inside iron or steel containers so as to by-pass or effectively short-circuit any interfering external magnetic field.

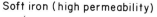
Soft iron (high permeability)

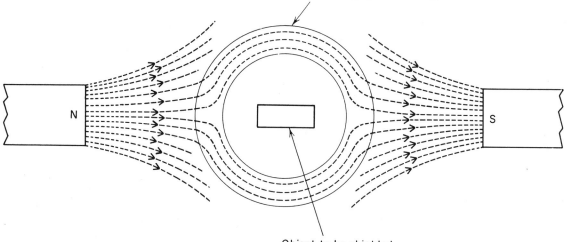

Object to be shielded

Making Magnetic Boats

69

Materials you will need:

1. *Cork*
2. *Six paper clips*
3. *Magnet*
4. *Nonmagnetic container of water such as an aluminum pie dish or a large plastic dish*

WITH a sharp knife slice the cork into little disks no more than ¼ inch thick. Glue a paper clip onto each of them as illustrated. If you have no glue, you can also attach the paper clips to the cork with hot wax dripped from a candle. The paper clip will be at the bottom of the boat, and if you wish, you can insert a toothpick on the top and attach little paper sails for a more realistic appearance. About six of these little boats will be enough to make a nice game.

Place the boats in the water with the paper clips on the bottom. You will find that you can steer the boats by moving your magnet near them or even under the water. No matter where you move your magnet, the boats will follow. It will make no difference whether you use the North or the South pole, because both poles attract equally. This experiment proves once again that magnetism will act through water and through the nonmagnetic material in which the water is contained. You can have a lot of fun with this magnetic navy.

If you don't have a regular cork handy, then the cork inside the steel bottle tops used on soda pop bottles will do very nicely.

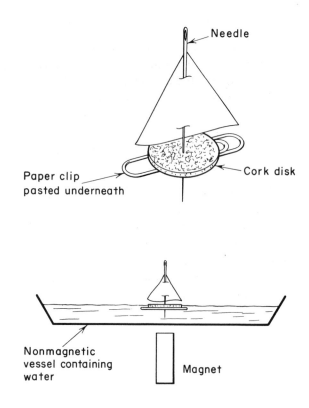

70

Magnetic Pick-up Sticks

Materials you will need:

1. *Dozen toothpicks*
2. *Dozen paper clips*
3. *Magnet*

FASTEN the paper clips around the toothpicks as you would fasten them around a piece of paper. To play the game, let the toothpicks with the attached clips fall from your hand so that they land at random on a table or other surface. Now use your magnet to pick up as many toothpicks as possible by lifting them one at a time. This must be done without disturbing the position of the other toothpicks. See how many you can pick up.

In order to give the game point values, you might color some of the toothpicks. As-

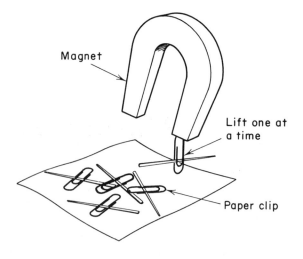

sign various values to them, such as 1 for uncolored ones, 5 for black ones, and 10 for red ones. See who can reach 100 first.

current electricity
and electromagnetism

We have already learned that there are two kinds of electricity. One is static electricity, dealt with in the first section of this book. The other is current electricity, which is the subject of this, the third and final section. We will find out how to produce, observe, and utilize electricity in motion.

Wherever a source of voltage is required, a 1½-volt dry cell (No. 6) or a 6-volt lantern battery should be used for longest life and best results. Both have screw terminals which make them easy to use. The lantern battery is recommended as several experiments require a greater voltage than that provided by a dry cell.

How to Make a
Current Detector (Galvanoscope)

Materials you will need:

1. *Compass (a 10 cent compass from a five-and-dime or toy store will be fine)*
2. *Small piece of wood (about 3 x 4 inches)*
3. *About 30 feet of insulated copper wire (any gauge from #20 to #26 cotton-covered or enamel-insulated will be all right)*
4. *Small piece of cardboard*
5. *Four thumbtacks*
6. *Source of current such as a 1½-volt dry cell or a 6-volt lantern battery*

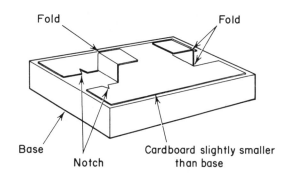

Figure A

ELECTRIC current is invisible and can be detected only by the effect it produces. Oftentimes we may want to know if a current is flowing in a circuit or if a source is capable of causing a current to flow. The sensitive current detector we shall now construct can do this job for us. It detects the presence of even a small amount of current and will be used in a number of other experiments.

In subsequent experiments we will learn that current flowing in a wire will deflect a compass needle. We will now "amplify" this effect by putting a number of turns of wire around our compass. Thus the effect of the current in each wire is added to that of every other wire. We will then have an instrument which is capable of creating a magnetic field that is greater than that generated by a current

over a single wire, and which will thus be able to indicate this current flow.

Construction is very simple. To make our instrument sturdy, cut out a little cardboard base as shown in Figure A. The exact size of the base will depend on the diameter of your compass. Wind about forty turns of insulated wire closely over the base and compass, leaving about one foot of wire before starting the first turn and after the last. Now wrap the two ends of wire once around each leg of the cardboard base and into the little notch, so as to hold the wires securely. The whole assembly (Figure B) is fastened to the wooden board with four thumbtacks. First insert two thumbtacks loosely on the side of the board where the wire comes out, and wrap a few turns of each wire (the beginning and end of our coil) around them. Then push the tacks into the board to hold the wires fast.

Let about ten inches of wire come out from each tack, and scrape off the enamel or strip the cotton covering from each of the ends for about an inch and you are finished. For a really professional touch, wind the wires into small helixes (spirals) around a pencil or dowel stick.

The 40 turns of wire increase the sensitivity of our detector by 80 over that of a single wire across the compass. We effectively have 40 wires over the compass and 40 under it; a greater or lesser number of turns will increase or decrease the sensitivity of the current detector correspondingly.

We know that the earth's magnetic field aligns the magnetized needle of our compass in a North-South position and holds it there so long as there is no current flowing in the coil. Any current in the coil around our compass creates another magnetic field, which, in addition to that of the earth's, affects the position of the compass needle.

For the best results, place the current detector in such a way that when no current is flowing, the coil is directly over and under the compass needle as it points North and South. In other words, the coil is placed parallel to the compass needle.

To test the current detector, connect one of the wires to one terminal of a dry cell or 6-volt battery, and touch the other wire to the other terminal. See what happens to the compass needle? The swinging compass needle proves that an electric current is flowing through the coil.

Now reverse the connections, and note that the compass will deflect in the opposite direction. The direction in which the compass needle is deflected depends on the direction in which the current is flowing in the coil.

The current detector we have built is a simple type of galvanometer called *galvanoscope* (both are named after the Italian physician Luigi Galvani, who will be discussed in

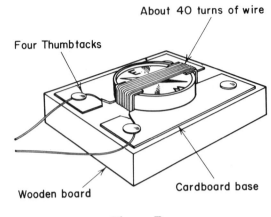

Four Thumbtacks

About 40 turns of wire

Wooden board

Cardboard base

Figure B

the next experiment). A galvanoscope indicates the presence of an electric current, whereas a galvanometer measures its exact strength. The movement of the compass needle shows the direction of current flow, and the amount of deflection tells us whether the current is strong or weak. Comparative current measurements can be made by noting the deflection for each source used. The greater the compass deflection, the higher the current.

Since the direction of deflection of the compass needle depends on the direction of current flow, and hence on the polarity of our current source, we can use our current detector also as a polarity indicator. First note the direction (clockwise or counterclockwise) of needle deflection with a source of known polarity, such as a dry cell, and accordingly mark the two leads + and − next to the thumbtacks. If two sources of current deflect the needle in the same direction, then they have both been connected with the same polarity to the terminals of our detector.

This current detector is similar in principle to many electric meters in commercial use in that it demonstrates that the more current that flows through a coil of wire, the greater the magnetic field and the greater its effect on the indicater used.

Make Your Own Voltaic Pile

Materials you will need:

1. *Pennies and dimes (five or more of each)*
2. *Five or more pieces of blotting paper or paper towels (1 x 1 inch)*
3. *Water in a glass*
4. *Teaspoon of salt*
5. *Teaspoon of vinegar*
6. *Current detector (made in the previous experiment)*

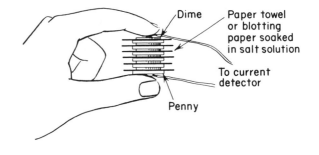

Dime — Paper towel or blotting paper soaked in salt solution — To current detector — Penny

AROUND the year 1780 a physician and professor of anatomy at Bologna, Italy, named Luigi Galvani, observed that some frog's legs he was cleaning twitched violently when they were touched by two different metals such as copper and iron. Galvani thought he had discovered a new source of electricity, which he believed to be "animal electricity." Actually, he had discovered, by accident, the basic principle used in making a battery to produce electricity.

Galvani's countryman and fellow scientist, Alessandro Volta, who was a professor of physics at the University of Pavia, decided that some mysterious action between the two dissimilar metals and the fluid in the frog's leg was actually responsible for the twitching, and finally concluded that the movement was caused by electricity generated by two dissimilar metals separated by something moist. He then set out to make the first electric battery.

Volta built a pile of zinc and copper disks separated by pieces of cloth, soaked in diluted acetic acid or in a salt solution. He found that the electric potential thus developed depended directly on the height of the pile; the higher the pile, the more electricity that was available. The pile could furthermore be used over and over again. Volta realized that he had made a device that could produce an electric current whenever it was needed.

This "voltaic pile," as it was eventually called in honor of its inventor, was the first electric battery. It made possible the generation of "current" electricity, which is to be differentiated from the "static" electricity we dealt with in our previous experiments.

Volta never knew precisely why his battery worked, but we have since found out that when we separate two different metals (called the *electrodes*) by a conducting liquid that acts more strongly on one metal than on the other (called the *electrolyte*), electrons move through the liquid, and the metal which is least acted upon is charged to a higher electrical potential than the other. An electric current can be made to flow from the metal with the high potential to the one with the low potential by connecting the two metals with a wire or other conductor. (This difference of potential is called *voltage*). A simple analogy is water going from a higher to a lower level by flowing through a pipe.

You can easily make a battery like the one Volta originated and show how the chemical action of two different metals produces electricity. We will use pennies instead of zinc and dimes instead of copper. We are not going to produce much electricity, but it should be sufficient to move the needle of the compass of the current detector.

Fold some paper towels or blotting paper into pads about 1 inch square (somewhat larger than a postage stamp), and soak them for a while in a salt water solution made by dissolving a teaspoon of salt in a half glass of water.

First let us make a single cell. Place a dime and penny on each side of one of the moistened pads, hold them as illustrated, and connect the leads from your current detector to the dime and penny. Make sure that the point of contact of the wire with the coin has been stripped bare of insulation. You will notice that the compass needle moves, thus indicating that we have a flow of current.

Now let us increase the potential by making a pile of pennies, dimes and blotting paper. Stack them as illustrated so that dimes and pennies alternate with a piece of blotting paper between each pair. About five pairs of coins should give you good results. Now connect the pile to the current detector again. Is the compass deflection greater this time? Now wet your fingertips and touch the top and bottom coins. Do you get a little shock? It's perfectly harmless. The voltage is greater than that of the single cell we made before because we are now connecting five cells together. The electricity from each cell is added to that of all the others. You can add many more cells to this battery (a battery consists of two or more cells) until it can produce very sizable shocks.

Now try the same experiment again, but this time use a tablespoon of vinegar instead of the salt. Which solution gives better results?

You might also try different pairs of metal to see which combination gives the best results. Try a penny and a dime, or a copper penny and a zinc penny, a piece of zinc from the outside of a discarded dry cell and a strip of copper, as well as any other number of combinations.

Always take the pile apart as soon as you are through using it, or else the coins will be corroded.

Flashlight batteries are very much like the one we make in this experiment, but zinc and carbon are used instead of the coins, and sal ammoniac and zinc chloride take the place of the salt water.

73 Getting Electricity from a Lemon

Materials you will need:

1. *Lemon*
2. *Paper clip*
3. *About 6 inches of stiff copper wire (not insulated)*
4. *Current detector*

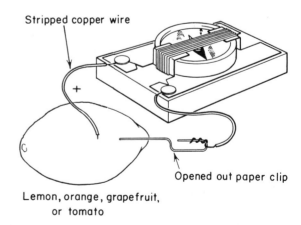

Stripped copper wire

Opened out paper clip

Lemon, orange, grapefruit, or tomato

WE can make another form of a voltaic cell by using a lemon. We know that a cell consists of two electrodes, separated and immersed in an electrolyte. Two different materials are used for the electrodes so that the electrolyte will act more on one electrode than it does on the other and thus produce a potential difference between them.

Here is how we make our cell: Roll the lemon on a hard surface with your palm so as to break up some of the tissue. Now straighten out the paper clip, and push it into the lemon about half way. Then take a piece of stiff copper wire, clean the insulation off it, and push it into the lemon near the paper clip. Both wires should be close to each other but should not be touching inside or outside the lemon. If you have any difficulty, you can first make a hole with the paper clip so that the copper wire may be more easily inserted.

To find out whether you have made a source of electricity, first touch your tongue to the ends of the two wires that come out of the lemon. You will taste a slight acidity on them. You may even feel a slight tingling. This is the same taste that you can experience by connecting two wires to the terminals of a dry cell and touching the other ends of the wires to your tongue, so we must conclude that we have produced a voltage by simply sticking two pieces of wire into a lemon. If you wish, you can also try this experiment with an orange, apple, or any other fruit.

Another way of testing whether you have a source of electricity is to use the current detector and see how much the compass needle deflects. You can test the polarity of the voltage by comparing the direction in which the compass needle swings with that you get when you connect the detector to a source whose polarity is known. You will find that the copper wire will be positive and the paper clip negative.

Electricity Can Produce Heat and Light

Materials you will need:
1. *Dry cell or battery*
2. *Four-inch length of picture frame wire*

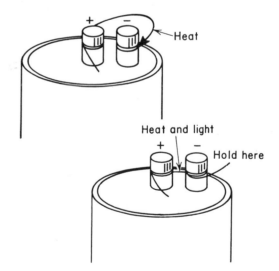

WE know from the toaster, electric heater, flat iron, electric perculator, and electric stove that electricity can be used to produce heat. If you would like to produce heat by electricity, try this simple experiment. Remove one thin strand of wire from a 4-inch piece of picture frame wire. Such wire is made of iron. Wrap one end around one battery terminal, and tighten the nut so the wire is held on securely.

Touch the free end of the wire to the other battery terminal, and hold it there for a few seconds. As soon as the wire begins to feel hot, take it off the battery terminal. You've produced heat by electricity. The iron wire we use gets hot because it is not as good a conductor as copper. The resistance it offers to the flow of current produces heat. This principle is used in all of the appliances listed above. Try various lengths and thicknesses of wire and various battery voltages (1½ and 6) to see their effect on the heat produced.

What would happen if we had a lot of current and the wire got hotter and hotter? It would become red-hot, perhaps even white-hot, and would give off light. This is the principle of operation of the incandescent bulb which was discovered by Thomas A. Edison. Let's try it.

Again use one thin strand of iron picture wire, and fasten it to one battery terminal. Hold the other free end so that the wire will go straight across to the other battery terminal and touch that terminal as illustrated. The short piece going from one terminal to the other will soon glow and give off light. If the wire is too thin or the current too high, it will quickly glow and melt. If it is too thick, the battery may not be strong enough to make it glow. The end you hold will not be affected since there is no current through it. Current flows only between the two battery terminals.

One word of caution: Don't leave the wire connected any longer than *absolutely* necessary because this is essentially a "short circuit" across the battery terminal. The battery will be rapidly exhausted and become useless if the short circuit lasts for more than a few seconds.

75 Electrochemistry

Materials you will need:

1. *Drinking glass*
2. *Some salt*
3. *Two feet of insulated copper wire*
4. *Six-volt battery*

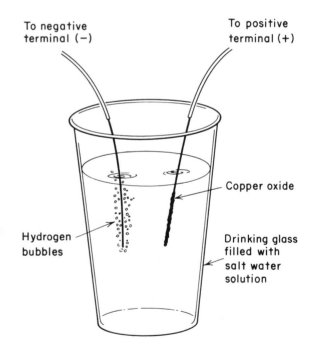

A very interesting experiment can be performed using a salt solution, a 6-volt battery, and some wire. We will be able to determine the polarity of the voltage which appears between two wires, and we will produce chlorine, hydrogen, and caustic soda.

First fill a glass about ¾ full of water and dissolve a good amount of salt in it. Insert into this solution two well cleaned ends of copper wire which are connected to the battery. You will see that bubbles of gas will appear at one of the wires (the one connected to the negative terminal). At the other wire (the one connected to the positive terminal) a greenish substance will be produced.

What we have done here is to break up or split the dissolved salt into its elements. Salt is composed of sodium, which is a silvery metal, and a greenish yellow gas called chlorine. To the chemist, salt is known as sodium chloride. In the process of splitting the salt, we produce sodium at the negative wire. The sodium readily unites with the water, forming hydrogen gas, and it is this gas which forms the bubbles by which the negative wire is easily recognized. The chlorine is attracted to the postive wire, where it forms copper chloride with the copper. The copper chloride then reacts to form copper oxide, which in time will show up in the form of a greenish scum on the surface of the water near the positive wire.

Thermoelectricity— Producing Electricity from Heat

Materials you will need:

1. *Current detector*
2. *About 2 feet of galvanized iron wire*
3. *Two feet of copper wire*
4. *Candle*
5. *Magnifying glass or a concave shaving mirror (for use if the experiment is conducted in strong sunlight)*

IN earlier experiments when we studied static electricity, we showed how we could get electrical energy by rubbing two dissimilar materials together. We thus converted mechanical energy into electrical energy. Here is another method of obtaining electrical energy, but this time we will get it directly from heat. This is called *thermoelectricity*.

In 1823 Thomas J. Seebeck, a German physicist, observed that an electric current is generated when two dissimilar conductors are joined and their junction point heated. This phenomenon came to be known as the Seebeck effect. We can very readily demonstrate this method of generating electrical energy.

You will need the current detector made earlier, a foot of copper wire, and a foot of iron wire (such as that used by florists for tying flowers).

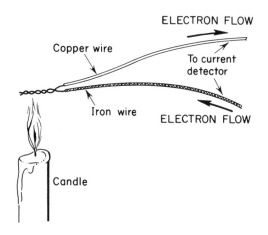

Figure A

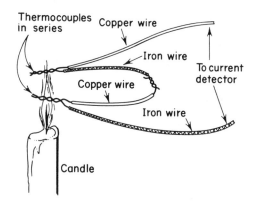

Figure B

Carefully scrape the insulation from about 1½ inches of the copper wire. Also clean about 1½ inches of the iron wire, though it usually doesn't appear to have any insulation. Wind the copper and iron wires tightly together for about 1 inch of their length. Use a pair of pliers if necessary to form a tight splice. Now clean the insulation from the other end of the copper wire, and connect it to one lead of the current detector. Connect the iron wire to the other lead.

Set the current detector so that the compass needle is parallel to the turns of wire around it. Now apply the flame from a match or a candle to the junction of the copper and iron wire, and watch the compass needle (Figure A). If everything was done right, the needle will start to turn slowly to one side, indicating that we have produced a current through the wire. As we know, the more the needle deflects, the more current we have produced. We have thus shown that when two different metals are joined together and a closed circuit formed, a current will flow in that closed circuit when their junction point is heated. Thus we have made a device for producing electricity directly from heat. It is called a *thermocouple*.

So far so good. But what if we want more electricity? Let us see what will happen if we make two thermocouples and connect them together. Again form a junction of copper and iron wire. Form a tight joint for about an inch, and connect this second thermocouple in series with the first as illustrated in Figure B. Now connect this assembly again to the current detector. Heat the two junctions simultaneously, and see if you get a greater deflection of the needle. When we connect two or more thermocouples in series, we have a *thermopile*.

Carefully watch what happens to the compass needle when you remove the candle flame from the junction. You will see that the needle will not immediately return to its original position (as it would if we had disconnected a battery). Rather, it will slowly turn back as indeed it had slowly deflected when the heat was applied. This phenomenon is a result of the fact that heat is not immediately absorbed or released. Therefore, since the junction remains cold for a brief period when the flame is first applied, it will take some time for the current to build up, and since the absorbed heat will keep the junction hot for a short while after the flame is removed, it will take a brief period of time for the needle to swing back.

Thermocouples find considerable use in measuring a rather wide range of temperatures. Instruments which make use of them are called *pyrometers*. In addition to the thermocouple, such instruments also make use of a meter which indicates the current produced by the thermocouple. This current, in turn, is proportional to the heat to which the thermocouple is exposed.

We can use our thermojunction and the current indicator to show that sunlight can also be converted into electricity. Here's how. Use the magnifying glass or the concave mirror to concentrate the rays of the sun onto the junction. If the sun is strong enough, the needle will begin to deflect. In order to be sure that this experiment works, you must keep the rays of the sun focused on the junction for at least a minute. Otherwise the junction will not have time to heat up fully. The larger the lens or the mirror, the better this experiment will work. If you don't care to hold the equipment in your hand, you can devise some sort of a fixture which will serve as a support and concentrate the rays of the sun directly onto the junction.

It would be interesting to experiment with thermojunctions made of various materials. You might try using copper wire and aluminum as one pair or aluminum and iron as another pair, and see which combination produces the greatest amount of electricity.

Potato Polarity Indicator

Materials you will need:

1. *One potato*
2. *Some insulated copper wire (to connect to the battery whose polarity you want to know)*
3. *Battery*

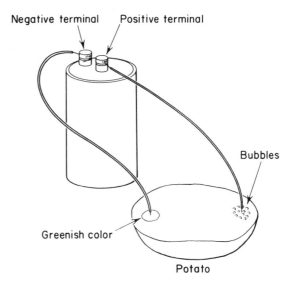

Negative terminal Positive terminal

Bubbles

Greenish color

Potato

SOMETIMES it may be necessary to determine the polarity of a storage battery, such as that used in an automobile or on a boat, because the markings have become obscured. When this happens, a potato will come to the rescue. Slice the potato in half, and connect leads from both terminals of the battery to the potato as illustrated. Put the wires about 1 inch apart so that they do not touch inside or outside of the potato. Also make sure that the part of each wire which goes into the potato has all its insulation cleaned off.

In a short while, you will notice that around one of the wires there will be green discoloration, while at the same time there may be some bubbling (or no indication of any activity at all) at the other wire. The discoloration is around the lead going to the negative terminal. The other wire, where the bubbles appear, goes to the positive terminal.

Electrolysis of Water

Materials you will need:

1. *Wide-mouthed jar or large glass*
2. *Two test tubes or similar narrow glass enclosures*
3. *Washing soda*
4. *Six-volt battery*
5. *Three feet of insulated copper wire*

SOON after Volta described his voltaic pile, two English gentlemen named Nicholson and Carlisle used his scientific discovery in this way. They connected two brass wires to a voltaic pile and inserted the other ends of the wire into water. They noticed that bubbles of gas formed on the surfaces of the wires. This was an interesting discovery, and it was soon noted that twice as many bubbles formed at one wire as did at the other. Before long it became clear that the water had been decomposed electrically into its two components, hydrogen and oxygen. This process, later called *electrolysis,* can be very easily duplicated today. Here is how:

Fill a wide-mouthed jar or drinking glass about half way with water. Attach copper wires to each terminal of the 6-volt battery. Clean the free ends of the copper wire, and insert

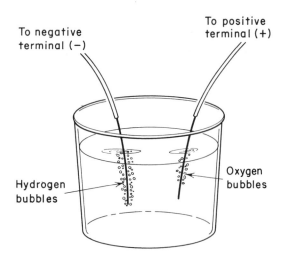

Figure A

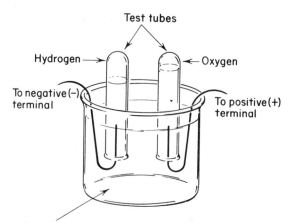

Figure B

them into the water, being careful to see that the wires do not touch. You will notice that some bubbles will form on both leads (Figure A), but the formation of these bubbles will be relatively slow. To make the experiment more effective, add about a tablespoon of *washing* soda (*not* baking soda) to the solution, stir to be sure that it dissolves properly, and reinsert the two wires. Bubbles should now form at a much faster rate at both wires, and you will note that the bubbles, when they become sufficiently large, will separate from the wire and rise to the surface. What we are doing here, of course, is to separate the water into its components, hydrogen (H) and oxygen (O) by electrolysis.

We can actually collect these two gases and show that we obtain twice as much hydrogen gas as oxygen. In order to do this, we need two small test tubes or glass jars which can be placed over the wires. Fill the test tubes or jars with the solution, cover the openings, and then invert and insert them, one over each bent wire, into the rest of the solution in the wide-mouthed jar. Figure B shows this clearly. As the bubbles begin to form, they rise and collect within the test tubes. Twice as much gas will collect in one tube as in the other because there is twice as much hydrogen in water, by volume, as there is oxygen. The oxygen will bubble from the positive lead and the hydrogen from the negative.

79

The Worm Turns

Materials you will need:

1. *Earthworm*
2. *Several sheets of newspaper*
3. *Six-volt battery*
4. *About 30 inches of insulated copper wire*

HERE is an interesting experiment that will show an earthworm's reaction to electricity.

Place the earthworm in the middle of several layers of very wet newspaper, and connect wires to each terminal of the battery. Now touch the other ends of the wires (with insula-

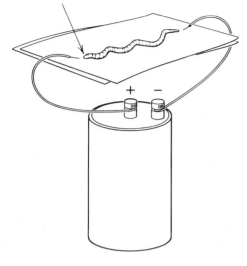

Positive terminal near head of worm

Figure A

+ −

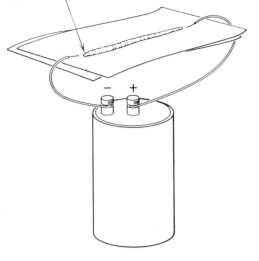

Negative terminal near head of worm

− +

Figure B

tion cleaned off) to the wet paper about 1 inch from the head and 1 inch from the tail of the worm. Note the reaction! Reverse the position of the wires and watch what happens this time.

When we touched the positive terminal near the worm's head, and the negative terminal near the tail, the worm drew itself together almost like an accordian. When we reversed the wires, that is, put the negative lead near the head and the positive lead near the tail, the worm had a tendency to stretch itself and be-

come elongated. Exactly why this happens no one knows.

It might be interesting to see what happens with only one cell of 1½ volts or perhaps three or four cells. Also, you might soak the paper in water in which a small amount of salt has been dissolved and notice what happens this time.

Fish are also known to react to electricity. Their characteristic reaction to a pulsating electric current is used to make them swim in one direction — directly into waiting nets.

Let's Make a Fuse

80

Materials you will need:

1. *Battery*
2. *Two feet of insulated copper wire*
3. *Saucer or plate*
4. *Small strand of steel wool*

A fuse is electricity's safety valve designed to allow a certain amount of current to

pass. It interrupts a circuit when too much current is flowing or when there is a sudden rush of current as from a short circuit. It must do this job quickly and surely. Its small size hardly seems to do justice to its great importance. If the fuse did not open the circuit, the excessive current would burn out the wires and cause injury or a fire. Let's see how the fuse works.

Lay a single strand from a piece of steel wool on a plate or saucer. Scrape off the insulation from both ends of two pieces of wire, each about a foot long. Connect one end from each wire to the battery terminals, and make sure that they are tight so that the wires make good contact. Now for the experiment.

Hold the other free ends of the wires in your hands, and touch them to each end of the strand of steel wool — the fuse. Flash! We "blew" the fuse. Actually it only melted quickly, because we made a short circuit directly from one battery terminal to the other. The fuse acted as an automatic switch by interrupting the circuit before any damage could occur. Had it not functioned, the wires might have become warm enough to hurt your fingers, or the battery might have been exhausted.

Examination of fuses in the home or in an automobile will show you that they consist of a short piece or thread of metal (the element) which melts at low temperatures and some sort of protective covering that keeps it secure. This covering also prevents any melted particles

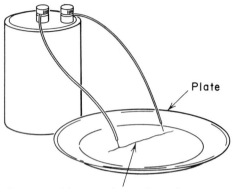

One strand from a piece of steel wool

from shooting out and thus doing damage when the fuse "blows." Usually the fuse is glass enclosed so that you can tell by looking at it if it is still working or has already done its job of protecting the circuit or the house from serious damage.

This electrical watchdog and lifesaver was invented by Thomas A. Edison, who patented it in the year 1880.

81 Relating Electricity with Magnetism (Electromagnetism)

> **Materials you will need:**
>
> 1. *Small compass (or the compass made in Experiment 53)*
> 2. *Three feet of insulated copper wire*
> 3. *Six-volt battery*
> 4. *Piece of cardboard*

ABOUT the year 1820, twenty years after Volta's invention of the battery, Hans Christian Oersted (1777-1851), a native of Denmark and professor of physics at the University of Copenhagen, made the far-reaching discovery that there is a direct relationship between magnetic force and electric force. He thus linked together electricity and magnetism into the new science of *electromagnetism*.

The discovery of the relationship between electricity and magnetism came about quite accidentally. Early scientists had studied magnetism and experimented with permanent magnets, but magnetism was considered a science quite different from the science of electricity. Oersted himself had originally believed that there was no connection between the two. To prove this to his students, he always connected a wire conductor to a voltaic cell and then placed the current-carrying conductor *at right angles* to and directly over a compass needle.

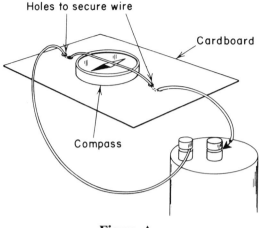

Figure A

When the conductor was in this position, it had no influence on the movement of the compass needle. During one of his lectures, however, he accidentally placed the current-carrying conductor *parallel* to the compass needle. The needle immediately rotated and came to rest in a position at right angles to the current-carrying conductor. He moved the wire around, and noticed that the needle would always turn at right angles as long as a current flowed through the wire.

Oersted continued his experiments and found that if the direction of the current was reversed in the conductor, the needle would still swing at right angles but this time in the opposite direction. He also discovered that

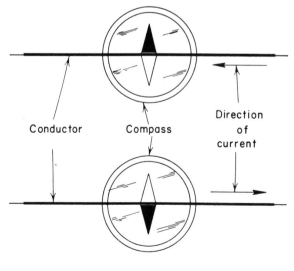

Figure B

when he held the wire below the compass, its effect on the needle was exactly opposite that he obtained when he held the wire above it.

After countless experiments Oersted recognized the magnetic effect of an electric current and realized that electricity flowing in a wire can influence other magnetic materials much as a magnet does. This basic discovery stimulated a tremendous interest in the new field of electromagnetism, and many scientists immediately set to work to develop and elaborate on Oersted's experiments.

We can readily duplicate Oersted's classic experiments with easily obtained materials. Here's how: Remove the insulation for about

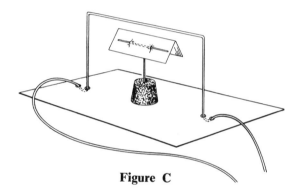

Figure C

an inch from each end of a length of wire. To make the experiment somewhat easier to perform, thread this wire through a pair of small holes in a piece of cardboard, and place a compass under the wire as shown in Figure A. Connect one end of the wire securely to one of the battery terminals, and then arrange the cardboard so that the compass needle points in the same direction as (parallel to) the wire. Now tap the free end of the wire briefly to the other battery terminal, while at the same time keeping an eye on the compass. See what happens? The needle immediately turns at a right angle to the wire. Take the wire off the battery, and the needle returns to its original position. Now reverse the connections to the battery, thus reversing the direction of current flow, and the needle will point in the opposite direction (Figure B). Take the compass out from under the wire. Straighten the wire, lay the compass on top of it, and repeat the experiment. Again

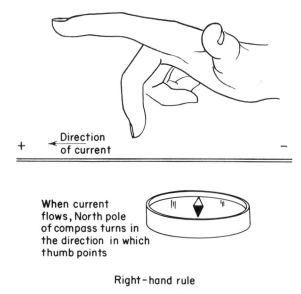

Figure E

When current
flows, North pole
of compass turns in
the direction in which
thumb points

Right-hand rule

Figure D

the needle will deflect, but in an opposite direction.

Move the compass away from its position directly over the wire, and see how far out the magnetic field will "reach." You will find that after a few inches there will be no noticeable effect.

If you don't have a compass handy (or if you wish to be a true experimenter), you can use the compass made in Experiment 53, when we magnetized two paper clips and pierced them through a piece of paper. This compass

will indeed serve as a good indicator. It is quite easy to place the current-carrying wire above and below this little device as illustrated in Figure C.

We can determine the direction in which the needle will turn even before we have a current. A rule of thumb for doing so was developed by the French scientist, André Ampère. Hold your right hand as shown in Figure D. If your middle finger points towards the compass and your index finger in the direction of current flow (we know that current flows from the negative to the positive terminal), then your thumb will point in the direction in which the North pole of the compass will turn.

We can add the effects of the wire above and below the compass by looping the same wire back so that it goes over and under the compass (Figure E). This time the deflection will be greater than that obtained when the wire was either above or below the compass, which shows that a coil is more effective than a single wire.

Magnetic Field Around a Current-Carrying Conductor

Materials you will need:

1. *Wire hanger (or stiff wire 2 feet long)*
2. *Compass*
3. *Two feet of insulated copper wire*
4. *Battery*

WE can demonstrate the magnetic field around a current-carrying conductor with another simple experiment. Make a stand as illustrated in Figure A from a wire hanger or a stiff piece of wire. Scrape the coating off very thoroughly for about an inch at either end of the hanger. Take a piece of cardboard at least 8 inches square with a hole in the middle

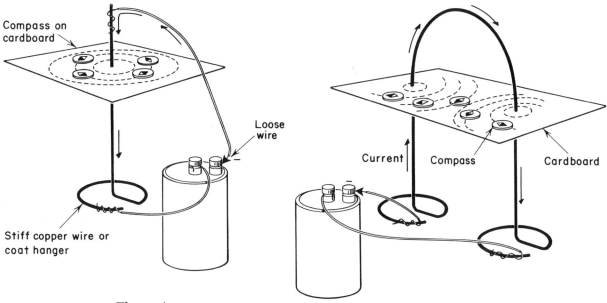

Compass on cardboard

Loose wire

Stiff copper wire or coat hanger

Current | Compass | Cardboard

Figure A

Figure B

and draw three concentric circles on it. These should be spaced 1 inch apart with the inner circle about 2 inches from the wire, which serves as center. We are going to use these circles as reference points for the compass to show the direction of the magnetic field.

Center the board on the stand so it stays about half way up without slipping down. This can be accomplished either by pushing the wire hanger through the cardboard so it will be held by friction or by making a little collar on the wire out of cellulose tape right underneath the cardboard.

Connect the stand with a wire to one terminal of the battery as shown. Lay the compass on any spot on the first circle, and tap the loose wire to the other battery terminal so that a current will flow. If the circuit has been connected properly, the needle will align itself in a direction tangent to the circle on which it lies, that is to say, it will point in the direction of the circumference of the circle at that point. (The wire should be held on the battery terminal only momentarily, because a very heavy drain is otherwise placed on the battery. If this drain is maintained for any length of time, the battery will be worn out very rapidly.)

Move the compass to another position on the circle. Again tap the loose wire to the free terminal, and note the direction in which the compass is pointing. Move it to a third, fourth, and fifth position all around the circle, and you will see that at all times the compass will be pointing in the same direction as the circumference. Move on to the next circle, and repeat the experiment. You will see that in all positions the compass needle will align itself in the same direction. In other words, the compass will point in a circular position around the wire on any of the three circles. This indicates that the direction of the magnetic field is a constant one, that it is located all around the wire, and that it spreads out from its center in a pattern similar to that which forms when a pebble is thrown into a lake.

At the extreme end of the cardboard or perhaps just a little bit further out, there may be no noticeable reaction of the compass needle as a result of current flowing through our little test setup. This is due to the fact that the strength of the magnetic field decreases rapidly as we go further and further away from the wire.

To show that this magnetic field is not located only at this particular spot on the wire, move the cardboard up or down about an inch or two. You will see that when the current flows, the compass needle will align itself in the same direction and with the same degree of response at various distances from the wire as it had before.

This experiment proves the presence of the magnetic field or magnetic envelope which surrounds a current-carrying conductor at all times. This magnetic field does not exist initially but builds up as soon as the battery is tapped (current flows). It remains there as long as there is a flow of current; as soon as the circuit is interrupted, it collapses and disappears without a trace.

Reverse the connections to the battery terminals, and repeat the experiments. The direction of the compass needle will be exactly reversed at all positions.

It is interesting to show the field which exists around a wire loop. Shape the hanger or stiff copper wire as shown in Figure B. Place the compass all around both wires at various points. Again a series of circles will be indicated, clockwise around one wire and counter-clockwise around the other. Reversing the battery connections will again reverse the direction of the magnetic field as shown by the compass needle's deflection.

83 Showing the Magnetic Field in Another Way

Materials you will need:

1. *Wire stand from Experiment 82*
2. *Iron filings*
3. *Battery*

USE the wire stand you built in Experiment 82. Sprinkle iron filings all around the wire where it goes through the hole in the center of the cardboard. Hold the loose lead (briefly) to the free terminal, and while you have it there, tap the cardboard slightly to permit the filings to move around just a little bit. They will align themselves in ever-increasing circles, the center of each of which is the wire. This proves, as did the compass in the previous experiment, that a magnetic field exists around the wire when a current flows through the wire.

Now tap the cardboard again after the lead has been removed from the terminal, and you will see that the filings will arrange themselves in a helter-skelter manner with no apparent pattern. Let the current flow again, and tapping the cardboard will, of course, cause

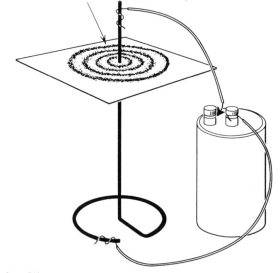

Iron filings (or steelwool shavings) showing magnetic field when a current flows through the wire

the filings to realign themselves in concentric circles.

In this experiment we show only the presence of a magnetic field, not its direction. Reversing the battery connections will produce a pattern that cannot be distinguished from the first.

A Wire Picks up Iron Filings

Materials you will need:

1. *Some iron filings or steel wool shavings*
2. *Six-volt battery*
3. *About 2 feet of insulated copper wire*

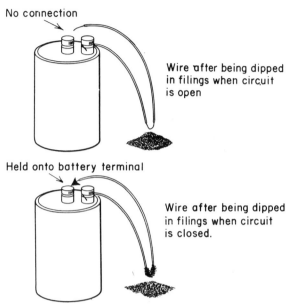

No connection

Wire after being dipped in filings when circuit is open

Held onto battery terminal

Wire after being dipped in filings when circuit is closed.

WE showed before that a magnetic field exists around a wire when there is a current flowing through it. If this is the case, then shouldn't the wire be able to pick up some iron filings much as a magnet does? Let us find out.

The iron filings you need you can easily get by rubbing a metal file over a nail or old iron casting. You can also use the steel wool pieces obtained by rubbing two pads of steel wool lightly together. Make at least enough iron filings to cover a dime, and place the filings into a little pile.

Clean the insulation for about 1 inch from each end of the wire, and connect one terminal of the battery to one end of the wire. Make a U-shaped bend in the center of the length of wire, and dip it into the filings. Lift it out again, and see if any of the filings stick to the wire. They will not. Put the same part of the wire back into the filings, hold the other end of the wire to the other battery terminal, and immediately pull the wire from the filings. You will see that this time a good bit of the filings will stick to the wire. Lift the wire from the terminal of the battery, and the filings will drop

off again. They will not stick to the wire any more unless it is again connected to the battery and a current flows. Don't hold the wire connected to the battery for more than a few seconds because of the heavy drain it will place on the battery.

What is happening here is this. We know that iron filings are attracted by magnetic force. Since the nonmagnetic copper wire itself has no attraction, it must have had around it some force which attracted the iron filings. This is the magnetic field we demonstrated earlier with the compass. Here we confirm again that we set up a magnetic field around a wire when a current flows through it and that the field disappears as soon as the current stops.

Checking the Magnetic Polarity of a Solenoid

Materials you will need:

1. *Ten feet of insulated copper wire*
2. *Compass*
3. *Battery*
4. *Large nail*

A FEW months after Oersted's electromagnetic discoveries were made public, Andrè Ampére investigated this phenomenon further. He made a coil by winding a long wire around a rod and noticed that when he allowed a current to flow through the wire and brought

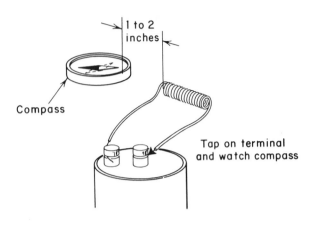

Figure A

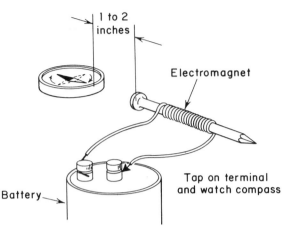

Figure B

this coil near a compass, the effect on the compass was much stronger than that of a single wire. He soon realized that such a coil acted very much like a bar magnet, since it too had a North pole and a South pole, which were located at either end of the winding.

We can repeat Ampére's experiments by winding our wire around a pencil, leaving about a foot of wire on each end. Slip the wire off the pencil, and you have what is called a *solenoid.* Clean the insulation off the wire for about an inch on both ends, and connect one lead to a terminal on the battery. Bring the solenoid near the compass as illustrated in Figure A, and tap the other battery terminal with the other lead. The needle will deflect, showing that it is influenced by a magnetic field.

We find that when the wire is coiled like this, the magnetic force produced throughout its whole length is compressed into a rather small space. Bring it closer to the compass and the compass will deflect more, but still a great part of the available magnetism will be lost in the air.

If you put a large nail through the coil, the magnetic field becomes concentrated around that nail, for we now have an electromagnet which we will discuss in detail in the next experiment.

Hold the coil with the nail in it the same distance from the compass as before, and again tap the battery terminal (Figure B). The deflection this time will be much more pronounced since we have concentrated or funneled all of the available magnetic strength in and around the nail.

A question comes up at this time. Does the polarity of the magnetic field depend on the way the wires are connected to the battery? Let us try to find out. Repeat all of the above experiments, but before you do, transpose the connections of the coil leads that go to the battery. This will reverse the direction of current flow. We will now attract the opposite end of the compass needle, showing that as you reverse the direction of current flow, you also reverse the position of the electromagnetic North and South poles.

To be able to tell the polarity of the magnetic field we use the "left hand rule." It tells us that if we wrap our fingers around the coil in the direction of current flow which is from the negative (−) terminal of the battery to the positive (+) terminal, then the thumb will point to that end of the coil which becomes the North magnetic pole. Therefore, if the current in the coil is reversed by reversing the battery connections, the polarity of the magnetic field will also be reversed.

Making an Electromagnet

Materials you will need:

1. *Nail (3 inches or longer)*
2. *10 feet of insulated copper wire*
3. *Six-volt battery*
4. *Some paper clips, tacks, pins, or other small magnetic objects*

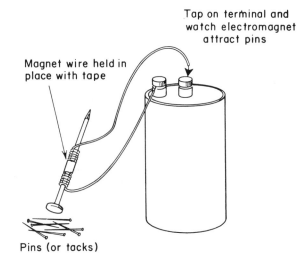

Tap on terminal and watch electromagnet attract pins

Magnet wire held in place with tape

Pins (or tacks)

WITHOUT question the greatest immediate practical benefit of Oersted's discovery was the invention of the electromagnet. It was conceived independently by Joseph Henry, an American Scientist, who was the head of the Smithsonian Institute, and William Sturgeon, an English physicist. Many scientists today consider it as one of the greatest inventions of modern times.

In 1825 Sturgeon bent an ordinary iron bar into a horseshoe. He then coated it with varnish and wrapped it with bare copper wire. When he ran current from a voltaic battery through the wire, the horseshoe became a magnet which was capable of supporting a weight of 9 pounds — quite a feat for that time. Stronger and stronger electromagnets were soon developed based on this principle.

It is quite simple to make an electromagnet. Beginning about a foot or so from the end of the wire, wind it around the nail, starting at either end. Keep winding layer after layer, always in the same direction, until about a foot of wire is left. At this point it is advisable to wrap some tape around the winding to hold it in place. Scrape the insulation from both ends of the wire, and connect one end to one of the terminals of the battery.

Hold the electromagnet over a small pile of tacks or pins, and tap the other end of the wire onto the other battery terminal. At that very instant, the tacks will jump up to either one or both ends of the nail, which now acts like a magnet. Take the wire off the battery terminal, and the tacks will immediately fall

off. Perhaps one may still stay on. Here's what is happening:

We showed earlier that current through a wire produces an invisible magnetic field. When the wire is wrapped around a piece of soft iron, the magnetic field magnetizes the iron by changing the position of its molecules and lining them all up in the same direction. However, when the current is turned off and the magnetic field disappears, then the molecules of the iron return to their helter-skelter position and the piece loses most, but not all, of its magnetism. What remains is called residual magnetism (see Experiment 49), which depends on the iron's retentivity (its ability to retain or hold its magnetism). Soft iron is used because it can be most readily magnetized and demagnetized.

Electromagnets are temporary magnets that can be turned on and off readily. If necessary, they can be made very strong. They are found in doorbells, door chimes, telephone receivers, telegraph sets, relays, loudspeakers, electric clocks, fans, refrigerators, washing machines, mixers, generators, circuit breakers, automatic switches. Cranes with lifting magnets are used for loading and unloading iron and for separating iron and steel from other materials. Electromagnets are also found in untold additional devices.

The strength of an electromagnet depends on the number of turns of wire as well as the amount of current available. You may want to prove this by doubling or halving the number of turns and testing the strength of the electromagnet by noting how many pins it can pick up at any one time. Also use two or more batteries in series, and note the increased strength of the electromagnet.

87 How to Show the Electromagnetic Field in Three Dimensions

Materials you will need:
1. *Floating magnetic particles (see Experiment 43)*
2. *Electromagnet (made in the previous experiment)*
3. *Six-volt battery*

Jar containing salad oil

To battery

THIS experiment is performed in essentially the same manner as was Experiment 43. There we displayed the magnetic field of a permanent magnet by means of small magnetic particles floating in clear oil in a glass or plastic container. This time, rather than bringing a permanent magnet near the container after the particles are agitated, we use the electromagnet constructed in the previous experiment.

The magnetic field is again shown by the position assumed by the metal particles. It will be very similar in shape to that produced by the permanent magnet, which shows us that the magnetic field pattern of an electromagnet is similar to that of a permanent magnet. The number of particles attracted by the electromagnet (or for that matter, the permanent magnet) depends on the strength of the magnet we are dealing with. (Be sure not to tap your battery for an extended period of time.)

Attraction and repulsion of magnetic fields can also be shown with the same set-up either by using two electromagnets or, to show an electromagnetic field and the field of a permanent magnet have the same characteristics, by using a permanent magnet and an electromagnet. To demonstrate attraction or repulsion of the magnetic poles, either reverse the pole of the permanent magnet you use or reverse the electromagnet's connections to the terminals of the battery.

How to Magnetize Your Screwdriver

Materials you will need:

1. *Fifteen feet of insulated copper wire*
2. *Pencil*
3. *Six-volt battery*
4. *Paper clips*
5. *Screwdriver*

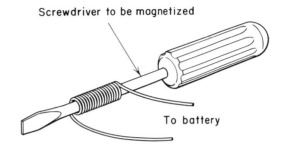

Screwdriver to be magnetized

To battery

BEFORE you start, test the screwdriver for magnetism by holding it against the paper clips to see if any of them are picked up. They won't be unless the screwdriver is already accidentally magnetized.

Scrape the insulation off both ends of the wire for about 1 inch so that the copper wire is exposed all around. Starting at about one foot from one end, wind the wire around the pencil to make a long coil. Every five or ten turns, hold the wire taut and push the turns together. Keep on winding until about another foot of wire is left. Push the turns together, and remove the pencil. This will leave you with a long coil of wire. Connect one end of the wire to the battery terminal, and then insert the screwdriver into the coil. Hold the other end of the wire to the other battery terminal, keeping it there for no more than 10 seconds. It doesn't matter which battery terminal is used for either end of the wire. Remove the screwdriver from the coil, and try to pick up some paper clips with it. You will see that it will pick them up, showing that it is now magnetized.

What we have done is to make a permanent magnet. That is to say, we have created a magnetic field which was more or less permanently imparted onto the screwdriver. After we disconnect our circuit, the screwdriver is still magetized. It will remain so for a few hours or a few days or a few years, depending on the material from which it is made. Since screwdrivers are made of steel and thus have high retentivity, they make good magnets and will hold their magnetism for a reasonably long period of time.

Unfriendly Paper Clips

Materials you will need:

1. *Three paper clips*
2. *Six-volt battery*
3. *Ten feet of insulated copper wire*
4. *Two thumbtacks*
5. *Small piece of wood*

USING the simple material listed above, we can illustrate in a rather interesting way some very important electrical principles. Starting about a foot from one end of the wire, wind it in the form of a coil about 1 to 1½ inches in diameter until about another foot of wire is left on the other end. Any convenient cylindrical form, such as a broom handle, can be used.

If nothing else is available, wrap the wires around two fingers. When the coil is wound, hold the turns together with two pieces of friction tape or cellulose tape. Scrape off the insulation from both ends of the wire for a distance of about 1 inch. Now connect one end of the wire securely to a terminal of the battery. Fasten the coil onto the piece of wood by bending the free leads and holding them down with the thumbtacks. Open one of the paper clips, as illustrated, to form a little hook at one end and hang the other two clips on it so that they are free to swing. Hold the two paper clips, which now hang close to each other, in the center of the coil, and tap the free end of the wire to the free terminal of the battery. See what happens? The paper clips fly apart. Since the magnetic field of the coil magnetizes both clips so that they have similar poles at the same ends and since we know from our previous experiments that like poles repel, the clips will push apart. Removing the wire from the battery terminal withdraws the induced magnetism from the paper clips, and they will once again hang down, one next to the other.

We show here that a current in a coil sets up a magnetic field, that this magnetic field induces magnetism in whatever magnetic material may be placed within it, and that like magnetic poles repel. Quite a lot of important

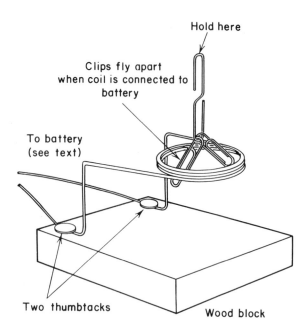

laws are demonstrated here with a very simple experiment.

The operation of certain types of electrical measuring instruments depends on this mutual repulsion between two magnetized pieces of iron within a current-carrying coil. The amount of separation depends on the current flowing through the coil. If we vary the current, we vary the separation. Conversely, once we know how much current it takes to achieve a certain separation, we can then indicate the amount of current flowing in a coil.

90   The Coil Moves

Materials you will need:

1. *The coil made in the previous experiment*
2. *Two thumbtacks*
3. *Six-volt battery*
4. *Small piece of wood*
5. *Powerful permanent magnet*

TO show the effect of an electromagnetic field on that produced by a permanent magnet, set up the assembly shown in the accompanying illustration. The magnet can be of any type, but it must be quite strong. A magnet taken from a discarded permanent-magnet loudspeaker will be particularly effective.

We have shown in earlier experiments that a magnetic field exists around a permanent magnet and that a magnetic field will be set up around a coil when current is flowing through it. We have also shown that the polarity of this magnetic field depends upon the direction of the current, so that depending on how we connect our battery, we will be able to set up a magnetic field which will be either the same as or opposite to that which is facing it from the permanent magnet. If we do this, let us see what will happen:

Connect one wire from the coil permanently to one terminal of the battery, and tap the other to the other battery terminal while watching the coil. One of two things will happen. When you tap the battery terminal, the coil will either be attracted towards the magnet and move down, or it will be repelled by the magnet, and move up. The way the coil moves depends on whether the field we are setting up is of the same polarity as the end of the magnet it faces. If it is of the same polarity, the coil will be repelled, and if it is of opposite polarity, it will be attracted.

Now reverse the connection to the battery. That is, connect the wire that went to the positive terminal to the negative terminal and vice versa. You will see that the coil's reaction will be the opposite to that it had before. That is,

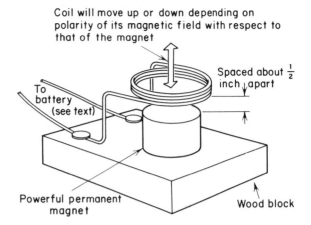

Coil will move up or down depending on polarity of its magnetic field with respect to that of the magnet

Spaced about $\frac{1}{2}$ inch apart

To battery (see text)

Powerful permanent magnet

Wood block

if the coil was previously attracted, it will now be repelled, and vice versa.

We have illustrated here the close equality of the magnetic fields, whether they have been created by a permanent magnet or by an electric magnet, and also the fact that the law of attraction and repulsion (which we proved in the section on permanent magnetism) also holds true for a combination of permanent magnet and electromagnet. This law is the principle of operation of over 99 per cent of all the loudspeakers in use today.

Magnetism Produces Electricity 91

Materials you will need:

1. *Current indicator*
2. *Bar magnet*
3. *About 6 feet of insulated copper wire*

IT was not long after Oersted showed the world that an electric current produces a magnetic field that other scientists naturally wondered if it was not possible to reverse the process and obtain an electric current from magnetism.

This question was soon to be answered by Michael Faraday, who was born in 1791 to a poor English family. He had little formal education. Though he started as a laboratory assistant at the Royal Institution of London, he eventually rose to become the head of this famous institution as the result of his brilliant discoveries and inventions. Faraday's most significant achievement was the discovery that a magnet can indeed be used to produce electricity. This discovery laid the foundation for the electrical industry as we know it today by showing us how to produce electrical power.

Many times Faraday placed a magnet inside a coil of wire and then looked for an indication on his current indicator. But he was always disappointed. One day in the year 1831, perhaps in a fit of impatience, he plunged the

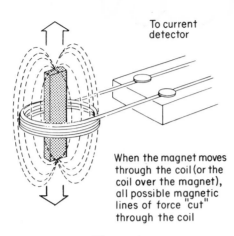

To current detector

When the magnet moves through the coil (or the coil over the magnet), all possible magnetic lines of force "cut" through the coil

Figure A

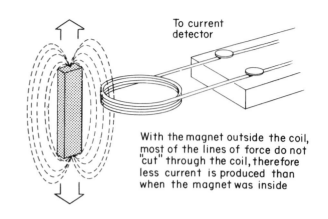

To current detector

With the magnet outside the coil, most of the lines of force do not "cut" through the coil, therefore less current is produced than when the magnet was inside

Figure B

magnet into a wire coil. As he did so, his indicating device showed that current flowed in the wire. He had discovered the secret. *Movement* of the magnet was necessary. The magnet itself did not produce electricity, but it provided the means by which mechanical power could be changed to electricity. Faraday caused the invisible magnetic field surrounding the moving magnet to cut through the wires of his coil. This very action generated the electric current, but to this day no one knows exactly why it should be so. We can easily repeat Faraday's experiment using a coil of wire, a magnet, and our current indicator.

Scrape the insulation from both ends of the wire for a distance of about 2 inches. Be sure that the shiny copper is showing all around. Starting 2 feet from one end, coil the remainder of the wire around a broom handle or other cylindrical object (even two or three fingers will do) whose diameter is larger than that of the magnet. Wind as many turns as possible closely together until you have again 2 feet of wire left on the other end. Slip the coil from the broom handle, and hold it together with a little plastic or cellulose tape. Connect the exposed ends to the current detector which we made earlier, and set the current detector on the table. Straighten the wires out so that the coil is at least 2 feet from the current indicator.

Plunge one of the poles of the magnet into the coil while observing the current indicator.

As you insert the magnet, the needle will move. Once the magnet is inside the coil and no longer moved, the needle will return to its initial position. Remove the magnet and the needle will again swing, but this time in the opposite direction. Here's what happened:

We have shown that a magnetic field exists around a magnet and also that a magnetic field appears to consist of a number of lines. These lines cut through the coil when you move the magnet. The result is the generation of a current (Figure A). This very important discovery is used in the electric generator, or dynamo, which supplies us with almost all the electric current used today.

Repeat the experiment, but this time turn the magnet around so that the other pole enters the coil first. The compass needle will now deflect in the opposite direction, showing that the direction of the current we produce depends on which magnetic pole enters the coil first.

To prove that it does not matter which of these two elements move, hold the magnet still and move the coil over it. The effect is the same as if you hold the coil still and move the magnet. Now let us try something else.

Move the magnet along the outside of the coil, rather than through the coil (Figure B). This time you will also generate a current. However, since the magnetic field seems to cut through only a portion of each turn, we will this time produce a smaller deflection, proving that we have generated less current.

You can also use the electromagnet made in an earlier experiment, Connect it to the current detector, and move the magnet across it (Figure C). Is the deflection you get greater or less than that obtained when you plunged the magnet into the coil earlier?

Be sure that at all times your magnet is far enough from the current indicator so that its movement does not affect the compass.

Try to generate more current (as indicated by a greater compass deflection) by the following means:

1. Making a coil with more turns
2. Moving the magnet faster
3. Using a stronger magnet

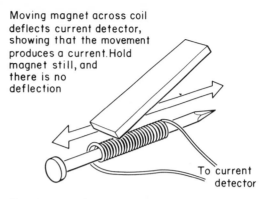

Moving magnet across coil deflects current detector, showing that the movement produces a current. Hold magnet still, and there is no deflection

To current detector

Electromagnet

Figure C

As you can readily prove, all the above factors have a direct bearing on the amount of current you produce.

Let Us Make a Transformer

Materials you will need:

1. Large iron nail
2. Current indicator
3. Ten feet of insulated copper wire
4. Bar magnet
5. Six-volt battery

FARADAY experimented further in the year 1831. This time he wound two coils of copper wire (which were separated from each other) on a soft iron ring about 6 inches in diameter. He connected the wires from one of the coils to a current indicator and the wires from the other to a battery. Then he noted that at the very instant that the battery was connected to one winding, the current indicator which was connected to the other winding showed an indication. When the battery was disconnected, the needle was again deflected

but after a while settled in its original position. Faraday named this discovery "volta-electric induction."

Then he conducted a second experiment. He wound the second coil right on top of the first coil, and he noticed that this time the effect on the needle was much stronger.

Thus Faraday discovered a means of transmitting an electric current from one circuit to another by utilizing only the magnetic effect of that current, without any actual contact between one circuit and the other. Here's why:

We have shown that a current through a coil sets up a magnetic field around the coil. In the previous experiment we set up a current by moving a magnet through a coil. Combining the two effects gives what is called a *transformer*. The current through one coil sets up a field which produces (induces) a current in the other coil without an actual electrical connection between the two coils. Let us try it.

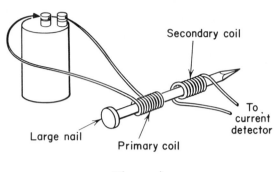

Figure A

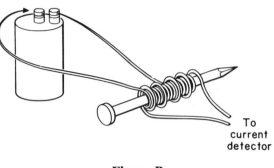

Figure B

Make a coil by winding about 50 turns of insulated wire around one end of a large nail. This coil through which our current will enter is called the primary coil. Now wind another coil of approximately the same number of turns next to the primary. This is the secondary coil, and through it our current will leave.

The primary and secondary coil together make up the transformer. Clean off the insulation from the ends of the wires, and attach the ends of the secondary coil to the current detector. Any current flowing in this coil will be shown by a movement of the compass needle. Connect one lead from the primary coil to one terminal of the battery, as shown in Figure A. Tap the other lead to the other battery terminal so that current flows through the primary coil. The compass needle will move momentarily and then return to its original position. Release the connection to the battery, and the needle will once more deflect briefly and return to rest.

Here is what happened. As soon as we touched the second battery terminal, current began to flow through the primary coil and a magnetic field built up around it. The lines of force of this field cut through the secondary coil. This action, which is similar to moving a magnet across the secondary coil, developed a surge of current. The moment the field reached full strength (that point at which it ceased to change), current stopped flowing in the secondary. Removing the wire connection from the battery stopped the current flow in the primary. The magnetic field around the primary col-

lapsed and again cut across the secondary coil, thereby inducing another surge of current.

The current flow in the secondary exists only when the circuit in the primary is completed (when the field is being built up) or when it is broken (when the field collapses). In order to make the transformer a practical device, the current in the primary must constantly change to vary the magnetic field. This variability is provided by alternating current (AC), the kind of current in use throughout most of the world today. This current builds up from zero to a maximum, then decreases, reverses polarity, decreases again to zero, and then the cycle repeats itself.

Transformers may thus be used to increase or decrease the voltage (difference in potential) of an alternating current. If a voltage step-up transformer is desired, more turns are used on the secondary coil than on the primary. If a voltage step-down transformer is needed, then less turns are used on the secondary than on the primary. A transformer is never used in a direct-current (DC) circuit, for the simple reason that it will not work.

We showed before that in order to produce the greatest possible current, as many of the magnetic lines of force as possible must cut through the coil. To prove this fact again, wind the two windings on the nail with the same number of turns but with one winding *on top* of the other (Figure B). That's about as close as we can get the two. Now tap the battery

[100]

again, and watch the current detector. This time the deflection will be greater than before. We use *closer coupling* to get the greatest possible energy transfer.

We can go one step further in our experiments. Let's generate our own current and through transformer action deflect the current indicator. Connect the coil made in the previous experiment to the two primary wires of the "iron nail transformer," and connect the secondary to the current indicator. Plunge the magnet into the coil (be sure you are far enough from the compass not to affect it), and the compass needle will deflect (Figure C).

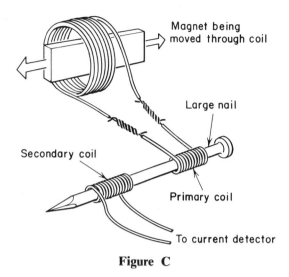

Figure C

How to Make a Lamp Assembly (Bulb Socket)

93

Materials you will need:

1. *Small piece of wood 2 x 6 inches (½ inch depth)*
2. *Two paper clips*
3. *Three thumbtacks*
4. *Two feet of insulated copper wire*
5. *Screwbase bulb (6 volts for 6-volt battery)*

FOR some of the experiments to follow we will need a lamp socket. A socket can be readily purchased, but it is much more fun to build one.

Straighten out the two paper clips, and at one end of each form a loop somewhat smaller than the diameter of the bulb's base so that the bulb will screw into this loop. Then, at the other end of each paper clip make a tiny loop which will go around the thumbtack which will be used to hold it in place. Scrape all the insulation off the head of a third thumbtack. Be sure that no paint is left. Also clean the insulation off both ends of two 1-foot lengths of wire, for a distance of about 2 inches. Wrap four turns of the cleaned-off end of one of these wires around the thumbtack whose head you have just cleaned, and press this thumbtack into the center of the piece of wood.

Now arrange the other two paper clips so that both large loops are exactly above this thumbtack in the middle of the piece of wood, and hold them in place with the other two thumbtacks as illustrated. Around one of these tacks, wrap the cleaned-off end of the other wire so as to make contact with the thumbtack and in turn to the paper clip. The shaped paper clips should be bent up slightly, so that you can screw the bulb in between them. The bulb will be upright when fully screwed in and will

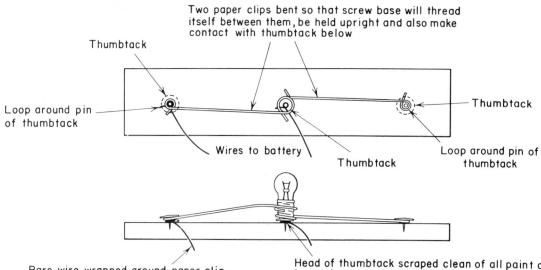

Two paper clips bent so that screw base will thread itself between them, be held upright and also make contact with thumbtack below

Thumbtack

Thumbtack

Loop around pin of thumbtack

Wires to battery

Loop around pin of thumbtack

Thumbtack

Bare wire wrapped around paper clip - both held in place with thumbtack

Head of thumbtack scraped clean of all paint and bare wire wrapped around its pin for connection to battery

make contact with the bottom tack. This may require a slight bending or adjusting of the clips, but you will end up with a very simple and rather effective socket. The wires that come out from the center and one side will light your little bulb when connected to a battery.

Make at least two of these pilot light assemblies for use in the experiments which will follow. Be sure that the voltage rating on your bulbs is that of the battery you use. We suggest a six-volt battery; therefore you will need six-volt bulbs.

94 Controlling Your Current

Materials you will need:

1. *Pencil*
2. *Flashlight bulb (6 volts or 1½ volts, depending on the battery you use)*
3. *Battery (6 volts or 1½ volts, to match the bulb you are using)*
4. *Four feet of insulated copper wire*
5. *Bulb socket made in the previous experiment*

WHEN a flashlight bulb is connected to a battery, a current will flow through the bulb which will heat its filament and cause it to light up. If we can control this flow of current,

we can then control the amount of light we will get from our bulb. If we have less current, we will get less light. In order to get less current, we must impede its flow by inserting some sort of resistance which will resist or impede the flow of current. Such a device is commonly called a *rheostat*. For our experiment we can use the lead from a pencil. Carefully remove about half of the wood covering of a long pencil with a pair of pliers or a knife so that the lead will be exposed.

Connect the circuit as shown in the illustration (by this time you know, of course, that you must remove the insulation from the wires where they connect to the battery, to the bulb, and to the pencil). Move the wire along the lead of the pencil. As you move closer to the

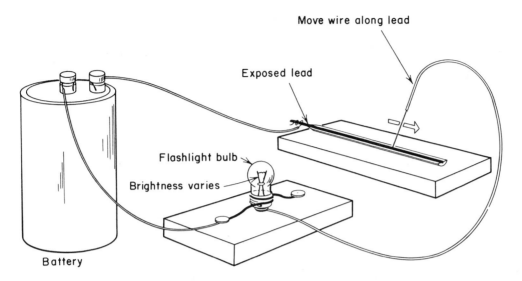

Move wire along lead

Exposed lead

Flashlight bulb

Brightness varies

Battery

point of the pencil where the battery is connected, the light will get brighter. As you move back away from this point towards the other end, the light will get dimmer. Here is why:

The lead of the pencil acts as a current regulator, or rheostat. It is a conductor of electricity but not a very good one. As we increase the distance of the wire from the point of the pencil nearest the battery, we bring more and more of the lead into play. This forces the current to travel a greater and greater distance through the lead. Since the lead is not a very good conductor, it therefore offers resistance to the flow of current. As we offer more resist-

ance, we have less current, and less current gives us less light.

The sliding rheostat principle helps control the current in radios to change the loudness of the sound we get from them, in motors to change their speed, in appliances to change their heat output, and in theatre lights to make them grow dimmer or brighter. Of course, current regulation in these devices is not achieved by sliding wire along a pencil, but the principle is much the same. The resistance element is usually circular. A sliding contact which is moved by turning a shaft varies the amount of resistance to be inserted into the circuit.

The Magic Diver

Materials you will need:

1. *Narrow glass or plastic vial of the type used to contain cigars, fountain pens, or tooth brushes (or a narrow test tube)*
2. *Small piece of cork*
3. *Small nail*
4. *Twenty feet of insulated copper wire*
5. *Six-volt battery*

HERE is an interesting little experiment that will prove to be a lot of fun. It does not require much material or preparation, yet it illustrates some electromagnetic effects in an entertaining way.

Clean the insulation from one end of the wire. Starting about 2 feet from this end, wind the wire around the center of the vial until you have completed about 30 turns, or, if you have already precut the wire, until about 2 feet are left over at this end. Again clean off the insulation. Give the wire about two or three twists to keep the coil together, and cover the winding with a little cement to keep it in place in the center of the vial. Once this is done, you are almost ready for the experiment. Make or find some means of support so that the vial will stand in an upright position. This can be done by cutting a hole in a big piece of wood to accommodate your vial. A base can also be made out of cardboard, a little box, or even a few books arranged so that they form an enclosure.

Now fill the vial with water to about 1 inch over the top of the coil. Insert your small nail into a cork that will fit into the vial, and adjust this little nail-cork assembly so that it will just float on the water. This will require a little work, and here is how you do it. To begin with, the cork must be large enough to keep afloat with the nail in it. Cut off portions of the cork, a small piece at a time, until the assembly will just float.

Connect one of your wires securely to one battery terminal. Then touch the other wire to the other battery terminal, and watch what happens! As soon as you touch the battery terminal with the second wire, the cork with the nail will dive downward in the vial and stay there as long as the wires are connected to the battery. When you take one wire off, it will surface and stay surfaced till the battery is reconnected.

Don't leave the battery connected for more than a few seconds, as this will draw a large amount of current from the battery and reduce its life.

Exactly how does our little diver work? We demonstrated in an earlier experiment that a magnetic field is built up inside a coil when a current flows through it. Once a current is made to flow through this coil, it sets up a very strong magnetic field right through the vial and

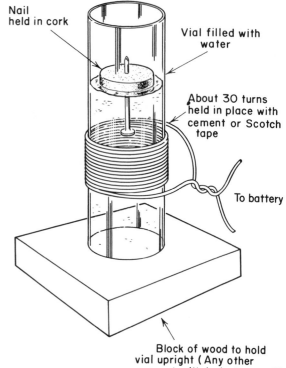

Nail held in cork

Vial filled with water

About 30 turns held in place with cement or Scotch tape

To battery

Block of wood to hold vial upright (Any other support will do just as well)

the water. This field attracts the magnetic nail towards it and makes the "diver" submerge. As long as the current is maintained, the field remains, and the diver stays under water. When the wire is removed from the battery terminal, the magnetic field disappears, and the diver bobs up again to the surface.

You can also try this experiment using a cork into which a paper clip or a thumbtack has been inserted. You may have to experiment a little bit with the amount of water in the vial and the size of the cork, but it will be well worth your effort. Also try what effect the voltage has by using a 1½-volt cell rather than the 6-volt battery. Also try to put more turns on the vial to see if you can pull down a larger, heavier nail. Also, try filling the vial up with more water to see if the diver will take a deeper dive.

How to Make a Switch

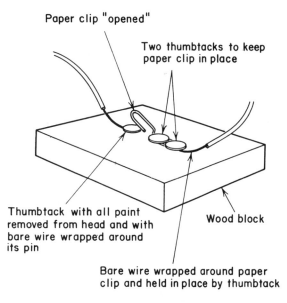

Paper clip "opened"

Two thumbtacks to keep paper clip in place

Thumbtack with all paint removed from head and with bare wire wrapped around its pin

Wood block

Bare wire wrapped around paper clip and held in place by thumbtack

Materials you will need:

1. *Block of soft wood about 2 x 4 inches (at least ½ inch thick)*
2. *Three thumbtacks*
3. *One paper clip*
4. *Two feet of insulated copper wire*
5. *Lamp assembly from Experiment 93*

CONNECT two wires from the lamp assembly to the battery; the bulb lights up. When one of the wires is removed from either of the battery terminals, the bulb will go out. When the connections to the battery are made, we have what is called a *complete* or *closed circuit,* and when one of the wires is disconnected, we have an *open circuit.* In an open circuit the current is not able to flow through the bulb to make it light. Though connecting the wire to the battery and then removing it allows us to turn the bulb on and off, it isn't always convenient to interrupt a circuit in this way. We don't turn our house lights off by removing a wire or turn them on again by reconnecting it. We use a switch.

Let us build a simple switch. It will be useful for our experiments and will also illustrate the operation of a switch very much like the one used to turn lights on and off.

Clean off the head (or surface) of a thumbtack by removing all the paint down to the bare metal. (As a final touch, you can use a little sandpaper.) Clean off the insulation from both ends of two 1-foot lengths of wire. Wrap one of these cleaned-off ends several times around the pin of the thumbtack, and push the pin into the wood about 1 inch from one of the edges.

Next, "open" a paper clip by simply pulling the "inside" out, as shown in the illustration. Don't completely flatten it, but leave the

larger loop standing up at a slight angle when you hold the smaller of the two loops down. To hold this smaller loop in place, use the other two thumbtacks. But first wind one of the cleaned-off ends of the second length of wire around the curved end of the smaller loop. Insert the two thumbtacks so that one of them holds this coil in place and so that when the larger loop is pushed down onto the surface of the third and cleaned-off thumbtack, it will make contact in the center.

The switch is now finished. The paper clip has sufficient "spring" in it so that after you push it down with one of your fingers, it will come up again. This very simple switch is called a *push-to-close switch.* You have to push it to close it, and as soon as you release the pressure, the switch opens again.

A basic switch consists essentially of two contacts which may be connected together at will to allow electrons to flow between them. When these two contacts are separated, electron flow will stop, and the switch is said to be open. Thus opening and closing a switch starts and stops the flow of current in a circuit.

Build A Conductivity Tester

SUBSTANCES can be divided essentially into two categories. First are the *conductors,* which allow electricity to flow through them with ease, and second are the *nonconductors,* or insulators, through which electrons will not travel or at best have a hard time getting through.* Among the insulators are glass, rubber, mica, silk, and oils. The best conductors are metals, but all metals are not equally good conductors. Some are better than others. Silver is the best. Listed below are a few commonly known metals in the order in which they rank as conductors.

1.	Silver	6.	Tungsten
2.	Copper	7.	Iron
3.	Gold	8.	Tin
4.	Aluminum	9.	Lead
5.	Magnesium	10.	Mercury

Conductors contain a large number of free electrons and therefore permit electrons to flow easily through them. Though silver is the best conductor, it is too expensive to be used commonly, so copper wire, which is considerably less expensive, is preferred for most electrical work.

When electrons move in a conductor, an electric current is produced. Such a current consists essentially of certain electrons pushing on other electrons that are free to move in the material in which the current flows. Those electrons in turn push others, and so forth down the line. Each electron actually moves only a short distance before it collides with another one; the one that has been hit then moves a short distance, collides with another, and so forth.

Nonconductors, on the other hand, have few free electrons and therefore allow practically no current to flow through them. In electrical work they are used as wrappings over current-carrying wires or as support for such wires. When nonconductors are used to keep conductors separated from each other, they are called *insulators.*

Let us construct a conductivity tester which can be used to test materials. Connect one of the terminals of the battery to the bulb assembly. One wire from the other battery terminal and the other wire from the lamp assembly are to be connected to our two test probes.

The test probes are constructed as follows: Clean off all the paint from the heads of two thumbtacks. Also scrape off the insulation for a distance of about 3 inches on the free ends of the wires connected to the battery and the lamp assembly. Wrap the wires (which now have their insulation removed) at least six times around each of the tacks. Then push the tacks firmly into the erasers of the two pencils as illustrated. Your tester is complete. To see if it functions properly, touch the two thumbtack surfaces together. You are completing the circuit, and if all connections are correct, the bulb will light up. Now separate the probes, and let us see how we can use our instrument.

Collect a number of objects which you want to test to see whether they are conductors or electricity or not. Here are some suggestions: A coin, a fork, a piece of cardboard,

---

*A new group of materials falling between conductors and insulators, called *semiconductors,* has been found to be of great importance in the last two decades. These materials made the development of the transistor possible.

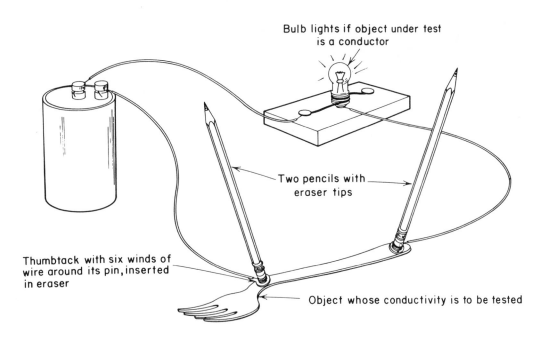

Bulb lights if object under test is a conductor

Two pencils with eraser tips

Thumbtack with six winds of wire around its pin, inserted in eraser

Object whose conductivity is to be tested

some nails, paper, cloth, rubber, a key, a piece of wood, a piece of tin foil, chalk, something made of plastic, a metal pot, plus anything else you can think of.

Apply your test probes to the objects under test, one at a time, somewhere along their surface. Be sure that you don't touch the probes' thumbtacks together while you touch the object under test, but keep them far enough apart so that any current which flows would have to flow through the object under test.

Here is what is going to happen. You will find that with all the metal objects the bulb will light, showing us that they are all conductors. With those objects that are not made of metal, or don't have any exposed metal surfaces, the bulb will not light up, and we see that they are not conductors of electricity. They are insulators.

Series and Parallel Circuits

98

Materials you will need:

1. *Two lamp assemblies (6 or 1½ volts)*
2. *Battery (6 or 1½ volts)*

ONE battery can be used to light more than one bulb, just as more than one light can be on in a house, all powered from the same source of electricity. We have learned that the path taken by an electric current is called a circuit and that any time we have a flow of current, we have what is called a "closed circuit." We will find out in this experiment (by means of our bulbs and bulb assemblies) that electrically powered devices can be connected either in a series or in a parallel circuit.

We will connect our bulbs both ways to find out the difference between the two connections. Two bulbs will illustrate the point, but you can use more if you like.

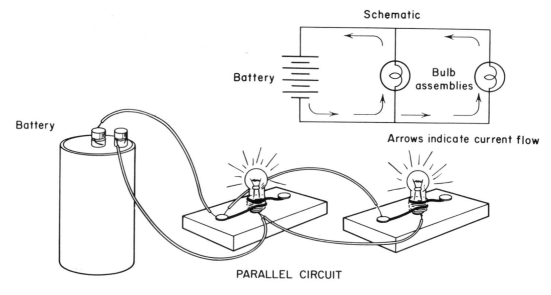

Schematic

Battery

Bulb assemblies

Arrows indicate current flow

Battery

PARALLEL CIRCUIT

Figure A

First connect the bulbs shown in Figure A. They will both light up to full brightness as soon as the circuit is properly completed. This is a parallel connection, that is to say, each bulb (or each apparatus) is connected directly across the wires that bring current to it. When both bulbs are lit, unscrew one, and see what happens to the other. It remains lit at full brightness, doesn't it? Screw the first one in, and loosen the other one, and you will see that the condition of one bulb has no effect on the other. That is, either one or both can be on or off independently of the other. You can connect more than two bulbs in parallel. Try three or four or more, and you will see that they all behave in a similar way. Each bulb can also have its own switch and can thus be controlled (turned on and off) without effecting any one of the others. If you study the schematic representation of the bulbs in Figure A for a moment, you will see that the current that flows through one bulb does not flow through the other bulb at all.

This parallel type of connection is used in the home for all lighting and appliances, such as toaster, dishwasher, washing machine, heater, motors of all sorts, etc. All of them are individually controlled because they are con-nected in parallel to the same two wires which bring electricity to the house (see Figure C).

Now connect the two bulb assemblies in series as shown in Figure B. Connect them to the battery, and again both will light up. Now as before, unscrew one bulb. See what happens? The other bulb also goes out. Screw it in again, and they both go on. Unscrew the other, and again both go out. Thus you see that in a series circuit the elements (bulbs) which are series-connected are very much inter-dependent. That is, what you do to one has an effect on the other. If you refer to the schematic diagram for Figure B, you will see that electrons must flow through both bulbs (or however many you use) one after the other.

You will also see that the bulbs do not glow as brightly as they did when they were connected in parallel. The reason for this is the fact that the voltage available from the battery divides itself across both bulbs whereas in the parallel circuit the full battery voltage was impressed across each bulb. Each will now have only half the voltage across it and will give correspondingly less light output than it did in the parallel circuit. If you use three bulbs, each will have only a third of the battery

[108]

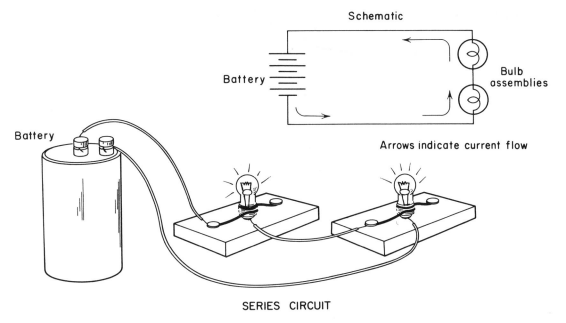

SERIES CIRCUIT

Figure B

voltage impressed across it, with a corresponding further reduction in brightness.

Some Christmas tree lights are connected in series. You may have had the experience of an entire string going out at the same time. What happened was that one of the bulbs in the series string burnt out and broke the circuit so that no more current could flow through the rest of the bulbs.

The bulbs which you use in this experiment should correspond in voltage rating to the battery. Don't attempt to use a 1½- or 3-volt flashlight bulb with a 6-volt battery. It will immediately be burnt out.

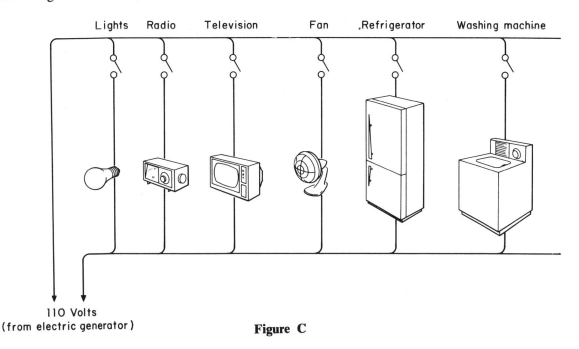

Figure C

Making a Telegraph Sounder and a Telegraph System

Materials you will need:

1. *Electromagnet (made in experiment 86)*
2. *Piece of wood about 2½ x 10 x ½ inches*
3. *Piece of wood about 2½ x 2½ x ½ inches (depending upon the size of your electromagnet)*
4. *Six-volt battery*
5. *Switch (made in Experiment 96)*
6. *Piece of cardboard about 1½ x 3 inches*
7. *Four thumbtacks*

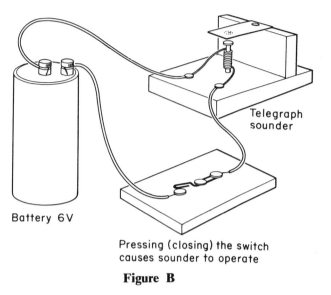

Battery 6V

Pressing (closing) the switch causes sounder to operate

Figure B

R ADIO and television are so familiar to all of us that we sometimes forget the value of the telegraph whose more than two million miles of wire are used to send messages all over the world at lightning speed.

Earlier means of communication such as the drums used among the natives of Africa, the transmission of flashes of reflected sunlight,

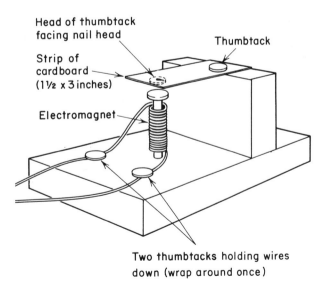

Head of thumbtack facing nail head

Strip of cardboard (1½ x 3 inches)

Electromagnet

Thumbtack

Two thumbtacks holding wires down (wrap around once)

Figure A

and the use of fire and smoke signals certainly leave much to be desired when we consider convenience, speed of transmission, privacy, and the distances that can be covered. The invention and development of the telegraph made it possible to send and receive messages in just a few seconds which previously took days or even weeks to reach their destination. (The word "telegraph" is derived from the Greek "tele," which means "afar off" and "graph" which means "to write.")

Samuel F. B. Morse, the eldest son of an American Congregationalist clergyman, was born in April, 1791 in Charlestown, Mass. Although a famous sculptor and portrait painter in his day, he is now remembered most for his invention of the telegraph, which made it possible to communicate by means of electrically controlled signals transmitted from one telegraph set to another. These signals are created by a telegraph sounder and then reconverted to letters and words by a telegraph operator.

The first long-distance telegraph message, "What hath God wrought?," was sent from the

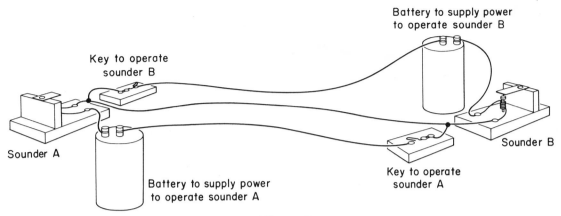

Key to operate
sounder B

Battery to supply power
to operate sounder B

Sounder A

Battery to supply power
to operate sounder A

Key to operate
sounder A

Sounder B

Figure C

United States Supreme Court in Washington, D.C., on May 24, 1844 to Baltimore, Md. The telegraph system was a success from that day on. In order to transmit all necessary letters and numbers using only two wires, a code was devised based on the number of sounds and their spacing. A distinct set of sounds and spaces was assigned to each number and to each letter in the alphabet. This code, called the Morse code, in honor of its inventor, is made of dots and dashes (long and short clicks).

A telegraph system consists basically of a telegraph key, a sounder, and a source of electrical energy to operate the sounder. The key is simply a switch which makes or breaks a circuit and respectively starts or stops a flow of current. When current flows, a magnetic material is attracted to an electromagnet, and when this happens, an audible click is emitted. When the key is pressed and released very quickly, a brief sound, called a "dit," results, and when the key is held down slightly longer, it results in a "dah," corresponding respectively to the dot and dash in the written form of the Morse code.

We can construct a telegraph sounder very easily and set up our own telegraph system. Here is how: In Experiment 86 we made an electromagnet by winding a wire around a large nail. Hammer this nail with the wire around it into the center of a soft piece of

wood, about 2½ by 10 inches. Fasten the two wires that come from the electromagnet to the board by means of thumbtacks, as illustrated. Push another thumbtack about ¼ inch from one edge of a strip of cardboard that measures about 1½ by 3 inches, and bend the pin over to keep it from falling out again. Fasten the other end of this cardbard strip with another thumbtack to a piece of wood which is about ¼ inch higher than the head of the nail. This is shown very clearly in Figure A. Fasten this smaller piece of wood (which now has the cardboard with the tack on it) to the larger strip so that the head of the independent thumb tack faces the nail head and is about ¼ inch above it. The telegraph sounder is finished.

Connect the switch and battery to the telegraph sounder as shown in Figure B. When you press the switch, you close the circuit and allow current to flow from the battery through the electromagnet. The thumbtack, as it is made of magnetic material, will now be attracted to the head of the nail. When this happens, you will hear a loud click. As soon as you release the switch, the thumbtack will snap back. Push the switch once more, and the tack will come down again with a click.

You can connect very long wires between the switch and the sounder so that they can be placed in different rooms. When you now close the switch in one room, you will hear a sound in the other room. This is essentially the sys-

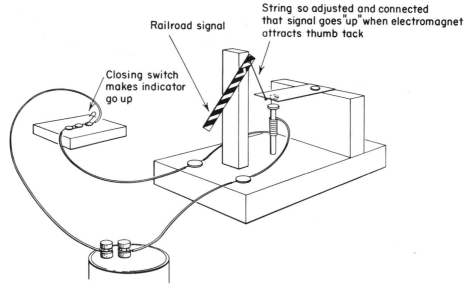

String so adjusted and connected
that signal goes "up" when electromagnet
attracts thumb tack

Railroad signal

Closing switch
makes indicator
go up

Figure D

tem that was used for transmitting messages at the time of Mr. Morse. Higher voltages and better constructed sounders made possible telegraph transmission over great distances during the latter part of the nineteenth century. Present-day commercial telegraph systems have been still further refined, but this experiment will indeed explain the principles upon which they are all built. If you make two sounders and two keys, you can transmit over reasonable distances with only three wires, as shown in Figure C. You can also use the telegraph sounder to make a signal for a model railroad, as shown in Figure D.

100 How to Make a Buzzer and a Relay

AN electromagnet is found in every electric bell and buzzer. If you have the chance to remove the cover from a buzzer, you will see it immediately. Usually, two electromagnets are used side by side for more efficient operation. You will also notice a set of contacts which are so arranged that the electromagnet becomes energized and de-energized many times a second. It will thus attract and repel a small piece of iron, which will in turn make a buzzing sound or cause a clapper to strike a bell to make it ring. To understand how a buzzer works, let us build one. We can

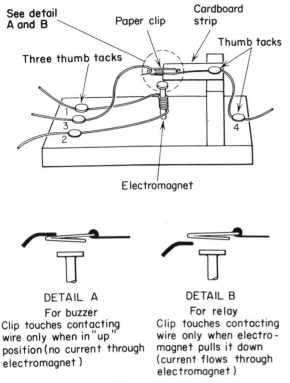

See detail
A and B

Three thumb tacks

Paper clip

Cardboard strip

Thumb tacks

1
3
2
4

Electromagnet

DETAIL A
For buzzer
Clip touches contacting
wire only when in "up"
position (no current through
electromagnet)

DETAIL B
For relay
Clip touches contacting
wire only when electro-
magnet pulls it down
(current flows through
electromagnet)

Figure A

strip of the same size. Remove the insulation from a piece of wire for about 2 inches on both ends, and wrap several turns of one end around the paper clip. Attach the paper clip to the center of the narrow side of the cardboard strip, and let it extend about· a third of its size over the edge, as shown in Figure A. Fasten this strip with a thumbtack to the upright piece of wood so that the paper clip is exactly above the electromagnet. This is important. The paper clip should be about ¼ inch above the head of the nail. Hold the wire from the clip in place with a thumbtack as shown at 4 in Figure A.

Now scrape the insulation from both ends of another length of wire, and put a little loop on one end. Shape the wire so that when it is held in place at 3 the loop will touch the *top* of the paper clip as shown in diagram (a) of Figure A. When you push the cardboard strip lightly with your finger, the clip should touch the head of the electromagnet, but when it does, it should not touch the wire from 3 anymore (a slight adjustment may be necessary at this point). Your buzzer is now finished. Connect to a battery and switch as shown in Figure B. When you press the switch, the paper clip will move up and down rapidly while making a buzzing sound. Here's why:

do this very easily by modifying the telegraph sounder made in the previous experiment.

Remove the 1½ x 3-inch cardboard strip which is held with a thumbtack to the upright piece of wood. We will replace it with another

BUZZER
Set up contacting wire as in (a) in Fig. A

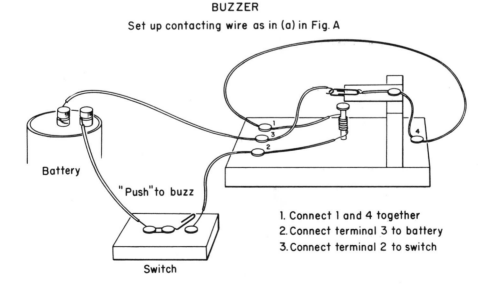

Battery

"Push" to buzz

Switch

1
3
2
4

1. Connect 1 and 4 together
2. Connect terminal 3 to battery
3. Connect terminal 2 to switch

Figure B

[113]

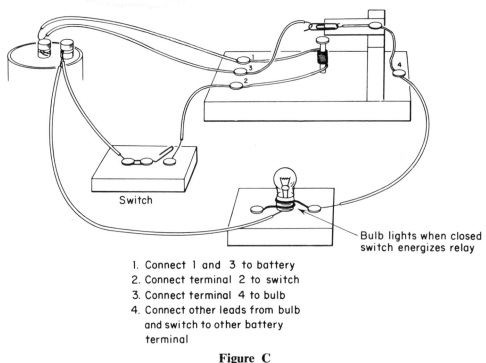

Bulb lights when closed
switch energizes relay

Switch

1. Connect 1 and 3 to battery
2. Connect terminal 2 to switch
3. Connect terminal 4 to bulb
4. Connect other leads from bulb
   and switch to other battery
   terminal

Figure C

Current flows from one battery terminal through the switch to terminal 2 of the electromagnet. Then it flows through the electromagnet to terminal 1, which is connected to terminal 4. From there it flows through the paper clip to the wire loop to terminal 3, and then back again to the battery. This current flow energizes the electromagnet, which then attracts the paper clip. As soon as this happens, the circuit is interrupted, and current stops flowing because the clip doesn't touch the loop anymore. When the electromagnet is de-energized, the clip moves back up and touches the loop again to complete the circuit, and the whole cycle repeats. It is this rapid up-and-down movement which gives us the buzzing sound. To make a bell, a clapper is attached to the moving part.

A relay is essentially an electrically operated switch which can be used to control the current in another circuit. Our buzzer can be converted into a relay with only a very slight modification. We just have to change the position of one wire!

To make a relay out of the buzzer, bend the wire going to terminal 3 in such a way that it touches the paper clip only when the electromagnet pulls it down, as shown in diagram (b) of Figure A. (Test this arrangement by pushing the cardboard strip with your fingers as before.) The relay is finished. When connected as shown in Figure C, the bulb will light when the switch is closed and will remain lit until the switch is opened again.

Here is what is happening: Current flows from one battery terminal through the switch to terminal 2, then through the electromagnet to terminal 1, and back to the other battery terminal. This energizes the electromagnet, which in turn pulls down the paper clip so that it touches and makes contact with the wire loop. The bulb is connected to the battery through terminals 3 and 4 of the relay in a series circuit. The relay thus acts as a switch which closes and thus completes the circuit whenever the electromagnet is energized.

For the sake of simplicity and to demonstrate the circuit, we used the same battery to energize the relay and light the bulb. Actually, any independent circuit can be connected to terminals 3 and 4. The relay will act as an electrical switch which will be closed whenever it is energized.

Four Games 101

Materials you will need:

In all of these games, the telegraph sounder, buzzer, or relay can be substituted for the lamp assembly. Materials you will need are shown by the illustration.

GAME 1. HOW STEADY ARE YOU?

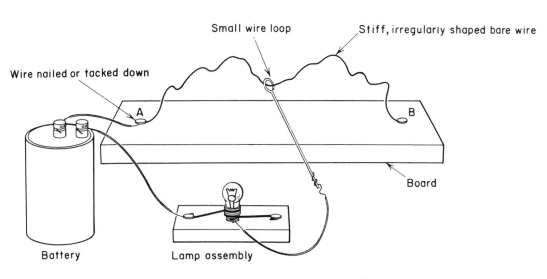

Rules:
    Start with loop at A. Go to B without touching the bare wire.
    If you touch it, bulb lights and you lose.

GAME 2. HOW STEADY ARE YOU?

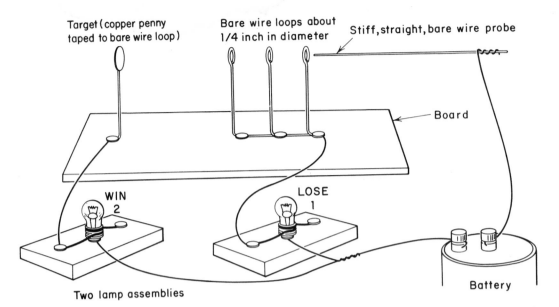

Target (copper penny taped to bare wire loop)

Bare wire loops about 1/4 inch in diameter

Stiff, straight, bare wire probe

Board

WIN
2

LOSE
1

Two lamp assemblies

Battery

Rules:
   Pass probe through the three loops and touch target without touching any of the loops.
   If you touch the loops, lamp 1 will light up and you lose.
   If you touch the target and not the loops, lamp 2 will light up and you win.
   If you touch both target and loops, both lamps 1 and 2 will light up and you lose.

GAME 3. TABLE TOP PENNY PITCHING GAME

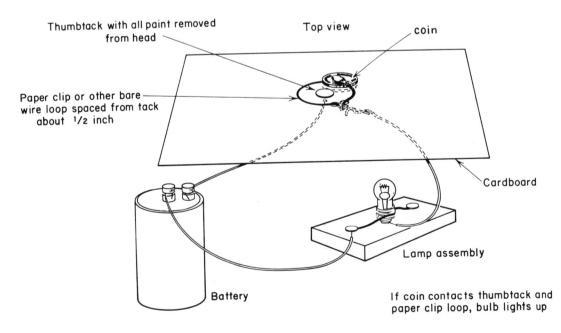

Thumbtack with all paint removed from head

Top view

coin

Paper clip or other bare wire loop spaced from tack about 1/2 inch

Cardboard

Battery

Lamp assembly

If coin contacts thumbtack and paper clip loop, bulb lights up

[116]

GAME 4. QUIZ GAME

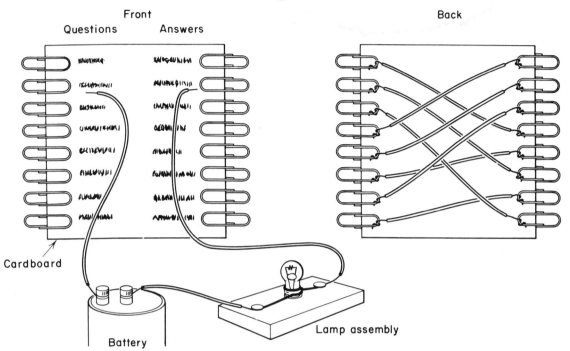

Two wires for connecting chosen answers to questions. If you are correct the bulb lights.